Women's Work in the Pandemic Economy

Myfan Jordan

Women's Work in the Pandemic Economy

The Unbearable Hazard of Hierarchy

palgrave
macmillan

Myfan Jordan
Grassroots Research Studio
Naarm, VIC, Australia

ISBN 978-3-031-40153-4 ISBN 978-3-031-40154-1 (eBook)
https://doi.org/10.1007/978-3-031-40154-1

This Palgrave Macmillan imprint is published by the registered company Springer Nature Switzerland AG.
The registered company address is: Gewerbestrasse 11, 6330 Cham, Switzerland

Paper in this product is recyclable.

For Ursula, Anouk and Piper; each a maternal gift.

Acknowledgements

Huge thanks to the many women who trusted me with their personal, and often traumatic stories of the workplace.

Thanks also to the Board of the Good Karma Effect for supporting the project with the provision of unpublished and de-identified survey data. All individual case studies and Facebook quotes have been sourced directly by the author.

Contents

1	**The Business of Caring**	**1**
	Introduction	2
	Employment Impacts of COVID	3
	The Care Frontline	4
	A Tale of Two Economies	5
	Culture and 'Imagination Infrastructure'	6
	The Importance of Caring	6
	Towards a Degrowth Imaginary	7
	In This Chapter …	8
	In the Next Chapter …	8
2	**Generation Expendable?**	**15**
	Introduction	16
	Changes to Circumstances	16
	Resilience to Change	17
	Changed Conditions of Work	18
	The Education Frontline	19
	Healthcare Services	20
	Worker Agency	21
	The Dual Discriminations	22
	Relationships and Workplace Culture	23
	Psychological Harms at Work	24
	What Wasn't Asked	26

In This Chapter … 27
In the Next Chapter … 27

3 The Toxic Workplace: For Women 33
Introduction 34
A National Culture of Bullying? 34
Pandemic or Endemic? 35
Neoliberalism 40
In This Chapter … 40
In the Next Chapter … 40

4 A Tale of Two Economies 43
Introduction 44
Gendered Bullying 44
A Bullying Predisposition? 45
History of the Gift 47
Gift Versus Exchange 48
Decolonising and Degrowth 48
In This Chapter … 50
In the Next Chapter … 51

5 Working by Gaslight 55
Introduction 55
The Social Glue 56
Virtual Caregiving 57
Good Karma 57
Methodology: The Gift Highway 58
Care in the Time of Corona 59
Material Gifting 59
Non-material Gifting 60
Seeking 'Non-material Gifts' 61
The Gift of Care 62
Beyond Money 64
Working by Gaslight 66
In This Chapter … 67
In the Next Chapter … 68

6 **A Hidden Gift Economy?** 73
Introduction 74
A Gift Economy? 75
Open Localisation 78
A Renewed Sense of Place 79
Free of Judgement 82
Frugal Abundance 83
Conviviality 84
The Gift of Time 87
Care-full 87
In This Chapter … 89
In the Next Chapter … 89

7 **The Unbearable Hazard of Hierarchy** 93
Introduction 94
The Gift Alternative 94
Bad Karma 95
Toxic Positivity? 99
Moderating the Gift Economy 100
Decolonising the Growth Imaginary 100
Reciprocity or Quid Pro Quo? 102
In This Chapter … 104
In the Next Chapter … 104

8 **Economy as a Gender Construct** 107
Introduction 108
A Gendered Economy 109
Men as Gendered 110
Individualism Not Collectivism 111
Corporate Feminism and the Girlboss 111
A 'Maternal' Gift Economy? 113
If Growth Is Patriarchal, Then Why Not (Re)matriation? 114
In This Chapter … 116
In the Next Chapter … 116

9 **Pathways Out of Capitalism** 121
Introduction 122
Masculinity as Radical Selfishness 122

The Care-full Workplace 127
'Imagination Infrastructure' and the Plastic Brain 128
In This Chapter … 131
In the Next Chapter … 131

10 Antiwork 135
Introduction 135
Rage Rooms, 'Screamatoria' and Dropping the Hot Potato 137
r/antiwork 139
Burnout 140
'Corporate Feminism' 141
From Antiwork to Degrowth 142
In This Chapter … 143
In the Next Chapter … 143

11 A Degrowth Reality 149
Introduction 150
The New (COVID) Normal 151
A Degrowth Imaginary 155
Horizontal Collectivism 156
Demasculating Men 156
A Degrowth Reality 158

Index 163

List of Figures

Fig. 2.1	Percentage of survey respondents citing known financial precarity indicators	17
Fig. 2.2	Case study: Ellie, university librarian. (Ellie's story was published previously in *Generation Expendable? Older women in the pandeconomy.* (Feb 2022). See: www.grassrootsresearch.com.au.)	23
Fig. 2.3	Incidence of bullying behaviours as defined under Australian Fair Work legislation	25
Fig. 2.4	Recorded incidence of bullying behaviours as defined in NHS Study, UK, 2013	25
Fig. 3.1	Case study: Margot, the healthcare manager. (Margot's story was previously published in The Power to Persuade (September 8, 2022). See https://www.powertopersuade.org.au/blog/the-disability-educator-a-case-study-in-older-women-and-the-toxic-workplace/7/9/2022.)	36
Fig. 3.2	Case study: Rachel, the disability educator. (Rachel's story was previously published in The Power to Persuade (September 8, 2022). See https://www.powertopersuade.org.au/blog/the-disability-educator-a-case-study-in-older-women-and-the-toxic-workplace/7/9/2022.)	38
Fig. 4.1	Health impacts of the 'toxic workplace' on women workers	44
Fig. 4.2	Genevieve Vaughan's core binaries for differentiating gift and exchange economies	50
Fig. 5.1	Membership growth in the three selected GKNs, 2018–2022	59
Fig. 6.1	Three GKNs: total pandemic keyword posts by 'gift economy' category	76

Fig. 6.2 Example: The collective decision-making and provisioning of the 'hive mind'. (Note, this example relates to no single author, but is a pastiche of GKN exchanges typical during the pandemic.) 81
Fig. 6.3 Case study, Carmen. (The comments/responses have been deidentified and condensed, but retain the intention of the writer.) 85
Fig. 7.1 Case study: Sandra 97
Fig. 7.2 Case study: Madelyn, a new single mother 103
Fig. 9.1 Good Karma Network 'A', total keyword posts by gender identity 2020–2021 126
Fig. 9.2 Good Karma Network 'B', total keyword posts by gender identity, 2020–2021 126
Fig. 9.3 Good Karma Network 'C', total keyword posts by gender identity, 2020–2021 127

CHAPTER 1

The Business of Caring

Abstract The early months of the global COVID-19 pandemic saw the concept of 'degrowth', and related theories critiquing capitalism, enter mainstream discourse. In Australia, COVID had brought mass job losses with particular ramifications for women. Dominating the 'care frontline', women workers in the sectors of healthcare and education were notably essential to society's continued function during COVID and also often faced significant economic and social outside of work. This book explores two economies of gendered work which took place during the first twenty-four months of Australia's pandemic experience. The first details the often 'toxic' work environments in the business of care. The second is a model of gendered labour that aligns with more 'circular', and what are often described as 'female-coded', gift economy behaviours. With a national culture which professes Australia to be a 'lucky country', one where everyone gets 'a fair go', this book argues that entrenched neoliberal tenets of individualism and meritocracy, combined with hierarchies dating from Australia's colonisation, work to punish feminised behaviours in the paid workplace while yet devaluing and invisibilising the freely gifted care women also typically provision.

Keywords Care • Gender • Women • Labour • Economy • Degrowth • Pandemic • Imagination infrastructure • COVID • Great Reset

M. Jordan, *Women's Work in the Pandemic Economy*,
https://doi.org/10.1007/978-3-031-40154-1_1

Introduction

In the early months of the global COVID-19 pandemic, 'degrowth' emerged from the cultural periphery to enter mainstream discourse. As an ontology long developing in academic and activist circles, degrowth was linked to the pandemic by the swift cessation of polluting practices that came as a result of 'economic lockdowns' to mitigate the spread of the new coronavirus'.[1,2] If media reports were a benchmark, it seemed that degrowth had at last perforated the 'imagination infrastructure' of mainstream culture, recognising and responding to an urgent need for 'systems change not climate change'.[3]

With what appeared to be genuine hope of a 'degrowth imaginary' arising from the pandemic ashes, news sources reported dolphins frolicking in pristine Venetian canals; elephants returning to Chinese villages.[4,5] Even cougars 'revisiting the streets' of Chile.[6,7,8] Bloggers wrote of emancipation from 'hustle culture', and the 'gift of time' was newly celebrated.[9]

In May of 2020, an open letter calling for 'degrowth principles to embody the global response to the COVID-19 crisis' had been signed by over 1100 individuals from 70 organisations across 60 countries. The letter asked humanity to 'radically re-evaluate how much and what work is necessary', singling out an imperative to 'emphasise care work' and to re-establish a wellspring of 'solidarity' through which we might disrupt a capitalism increasingly characterised by individualism, competition and greed.[10,11,12]

In November, the World Economic Forum (WEF) released a paper outlining the 'building blocks' of a post-crisis 'great reset'. The WEF paper also highlighted the urgent need to pivot from a 'growth mindset' and identify 'new metrics' through which humanity might measure 'what matters'.[13]

In the context of the coronavirus and related 'polycrises' of late-stage capitalism, degrowth, once little more than a loosely aligned cluster of theories critiquing capitalism, gained momentum; uniting 'commoning' philosophies with climate activism, decolonial and eco-feminisms, and other philosophies which seek to deconstruct or 'radically attack the economic growth paradigm at centre of our civilisation'.[14,15]

The 'degrowth' news stories turned out to be exaggerated however; the 'record drop' in carbon emissions short-lived.[16] What was heralded as an emergent degrowth was in fact the opposite:

> The ravages of COVID-19 do not represent degrowth worlds strived for by social movements. Yes, the health crisis has provoked declines in natural resources used and waste generated … And yes, the lives of some people have slowed down, as ambitious schedules give way to more time for reflection and relationships. But no, unevenly-suffered trauma, impoverishment, and death are not features of degrowth; on the contrary.[17]

As in other countries, governments in Australia responded to the rapid spread of 'COVID', by mandating economic lockdowns. In Naarm (Melbourne), the first city with a serious outbreak, lockdown measures were introduced early in 2020 and continued intermittently until October 2021, shutting down all but essential services. With schools and office blocks seen as a 'petri dish' for contagion, Naarm underwent massive social transformation as workers and pupils moved home to work remotely.[18,19,20]

Restrictions on movement affected all areas of life. Residents were allowed out for only one hour per day and one 'essential' shopping expedition a week, in what was portrayed—incorrectly it turned out—as the 'most locked down city in the world'.[21,22]

Employment Impacts of COVID

As with other countries, COVID brought mass job losses to Australia, with younger workers first impacted. Employed 'casually' and in customer-facing sectors, 38% of the Australians who lost work in the first months of the pandemic were aged under 25.[23,24]

It was soon also clear that the economic ramifications of this 'historic rupture' had a *gendered* dimension.[25,26] Routinely balancing low paid and casual/part-time employment with the unpaid 'reproductive work' of the home, economic analysts soon noted that a majority of job losses in Australia were positions held by women.[27] More than 100,000 Australian women exited the labour market between February and July 2020, with overall workforce participation for women falling to 60% in 2020, compared with 70% workforce participation for men.[28]

Women were not only losing their jobs through redundancy it transpired, many were also forced into *relinquishing* employment—and/or tertiary studies—to meet the extra 'domestic' burden resulting from the pandemic and lockdown conditions. The loss of financial autonomy saw many women newly dependent on male partners, who were now working—or unemployed or furloughed—from home, resulting in soaring rates of family violence, in addition to gendered economic impacts.[29,30] Before long, analysts the world over were describing a 'shecession' or 'pink recession', one with potentially long-term implications.[31,32]

Unsurprisingly then, the Australian Bureau of Statistics (ABS), reported half of all Australian women aged between 25 and 31, and 35% of those aged 42–47, had experienced 'high stress' during the first 6 months of Australia's pandemic.[33] For many Australian women, the pandemic only heightened an already unequal 'burden' of caregiving, and left them more economically vulnerable and dependent upon men.

As Australian economist Leonora Risse observed in April 2020:

> The undervaluation of care is a major factor driving gender inequalities in economic and social outcomes. Based on the way our society has been engineered, altruism, generosity, compassion and community-mindedness do not neatly equate to wealth, power, authority and status – despite being the invisible glue holding society together.[34]

The Care Frontline

While men dominated some of the suddenly 'essential' occupations under COVID, the care frontline of education and healthcare provision, aged- and child-care, community and home support for people with care needs, couldn't be put into hiatus while governments debated protective pandemic measures.[35] As part of the 'foundational economy', care work is essential to society's function and became especially so in the time of COVID.[36,37]

While early discussion of the pink recession had rightly focused on younger mothers, the impacts upon 'older' women were also important.[38] With Australian women already vulnerable to a 'gendered ageing' characterised by poverty, and even later-life homelessness, I commenced a snapshot study of work outcomes targeting women aged over 40 during 2020 and 2021.[39,40,41] This *Generation Expendable?* study ran initially as a survey across social media between March 2020 and June 2021 and was followed by interviews with a number of self-selected participants.

The aim of the research was to flag trends in the pandemic experiences of older Australian women from which future research might perhaps follow. With a working hypothesis that older women workers might be more 'expendable' in a precarious labour market by virture of the 'dual discriminations' of sexism and ageism, the study was designed to not only capture women's employment outcomes, but also to provide a platform for less heard voices.

A Tale of Two Economies

While this book is chiefly about women workers during 'COVID', it is more properly *a tale of two economies*. The first of these depicts the 'toxic' workplace environments of late-stage capitalism during the pandemic most particularly the feminised *businesses of care*.

The second economy presented is one which I will argue more closely aligns with the 'circular' economic models championed by many degrowth advocates, by decolonial and Indigenous thinkers, and also by many feminists. This model is recorded in a second study I conducted, again focused on gendered labour in the pandemic but research which recorded markedly different outcomes, work cultures and workplace behaviours to those seen in the *Generation Expendable?* study.

The Gift Highway study focused on three 'hyper-local digital sharing platforms', recording and recounting 'economic behaviours' of care provisioning occurring in online settings during the pandemic; behaviours which, I argue, align closely with what are often characterised—not without challenge—as being more 'feminine' *gift economy* practices.

As an alternative economic paradigm, gift economy models have become increasingly central to anticapitalist and feminist epistemologies. As Peggy Antrobus explains:

> In capitalism, the values of patriarchy - competition, hierarchy, domination - have been united with the values of the market. Money, together with the process of exchange, influences our thinking; making us concerned with equations, measurement, judgments of value, hierarchical categorizations, and quantifications of punishment and reprisal.[42]

Yet it was the 'social glue' of unpaid support, of care and human connection typically invisibilised under growth capitalism, that became acutely important in the context of a global health care crisis:

> It's inaccurate to measure the slowdown in production simply in terms of lost income and jobs in the formal labour market. Such an assessment is based on the judgement that economic activity only counts if it involves a formal monetary transaction. Behind the scenes right now, there are still millions of hours of unpaid and voluntary work taking place within our homes and communities. People are still caring for children, caring for elderly family members and people with disabilities, checking on neighbours, looking after sick family members, cleaning their homes, doing the washing, preparing meals, stepping in as substitute teachers for their children, and providing emotional support to one another.[43]

Culture and 'Imagination Infrastructure'

How Australians like to see and describe ourselves, the cultural myths which reinforce our national identity and which we (re)produce in our mainstream media and tourism narratives, also serve to uphold our internal national culture. Some stem from historical events such as the ANZAC story and that legend of the Eureka Stockade, the latter characterised as 'one of the most important moments of true representative democracy in Australia, when the people demanded the opportunity to be included.'[44,45]

In the twentieth century, these cultural narratives helped distinguish Australia from the British 'Mother Country' and to establish a quintessentially *Australian* identity of 'the lucky country' where everyone gets 'a fair go'. These cultural myths, a sort of collective 'imagination infrastructure', have, in the 21st century strongly fused with neoliberal tenets around individualism and meritocracy, creating workplace cultures where efficiency and a (solid) work ethic reign, despite oft-espoused values of 'teamwork' and 'equalities'.[46]

Even in modern Australia, our colonial legacy endures to shape life-course outcomes for a highly diverse population, many excluded from secure and decent work by dint of their Indigenous status, their race, age, (dis)ability, and the many other 'value propositions' and intersections of identity which structure Australia's labour market and workplace cultures: cultural settings which also still render caregiving as intrinsically linked to female gender.[47]

The Importance of Caring

While women/gender are the subject of this book, they are not the sole object. Rather, this is a book which depicts caregiving as both culturally embedded but also fundamentally shaped by the broader economic structures in which it takes place.

Understanding '*"the economy" is as much a cultural site as … the family, the school, and the community*', the two studies compared and analysed in this book offer proof that '*economic activities are always culturally inflected or embedded … There is no way they could be conducted independently of systems of meanings and norms*'.[48]

As Erella Shadmi tells us, the exchange economy of modern capitalism:

> [m]akes [women] blind to the needs of the other and turns us inward towards our own needs and individuality, constantly engaged in an endless

competition over career, success and capital, expecting that our value will be judged, usually in money terms, and thus will make our lives meaningful. It is as if we are always waiting for someone to recognize us and give us our just worth, so we can have an identity and meaning.[49]

By contrasting two distinct economies of gendered caregiving, I show how the cardinal essence of care is routinely conflicted within the linear meritocracies of the modern capitalist state. That, as well as rewarding the 'masculation' of women workers, hierarchies which structure the typical Australian workplace are not only 'toxic' for women workers, but also have negative consequences for 'care recipients'.

By contrast, care 'delivered' outside of exchange capitalism demonstrates a very different logic. Typically devalued and obscured by representations of economic 'growth', women's unpaid work—like the extracted resources of nature—is, paradoxically, the gift upon which capitalism depends.

Towards a Degrowth Imaginary

While the pandemic may not (yet) have proved to be the catalyst which will pivot humanity towards 'just and sustainable ways' of living, there is some evidence of increased awareness and interest in the 'new economy' alternatives either emerging or further developing as a result of the crisis.[50] For many activists, scholars and thinkers, a '*degrowth imaginary*' is comprehensively starting to take shape, presenting a paradigmatic alternative to the polycrises of neo-patriarchal, economic fundamentalism.[51]

The 'exchange logic' of 'free market' capitalism has us believe that all human behaviour is economic. That our decision-making, and activities of provisioning and consumption, rely 'rationally' on that which promotes and protects our own best interests. This has led us to a place where individual profit and related 'ego-oriented' outcomes now commonly take precedence over the collective good.

Our social systems have been set up an expectation of quid pro quo, a *transactional* paradigm in which the exchange equivalent commodifies almost all of human activity as well as our planet's finite resources. Self-rewarding 'economic behaviours' are said to be underpinned by heuristics which routinely default our decision-making to ask, 'what's in it for me?', driving a dynamism of accumulation and material excess which mounts an almost impossible—albeit existential challenge.

While the outlook may seem bleak, the findings of this book show that alternative ways of social and economic organisation are not only possible, but *hiding in plain sight*. For one 'economy' of women workers depicted in this book, the pandemic proved a time of trauma and psychological risk. For the other, an economy of care provisioning taking place beyond money, and outside of Australia's typically rigid and hierarchical workplace systems, we will see that collective and 'care-full' values—*economic behaviours*—where able not only to respond to the coronavirus crisis in female-coded' ways, but also to thrive in ways that are typically invisibilised under a patriarchal capitalism that not only disadvantages non-masculine genders, but also often men.

By exploring models of women's work in the time of corona through ontologies of degrowth, decolonial feminisms and gift economy theory, the evidence presented here provides both hope and proof that alternative ways of living have already emerged and can endure.

As Heide Goettner-Abendroth explains:

> We need not to invent an abstract utopia to find social structures which would embody the value of motherliness and the practise of gift giving they cause. They have existed over the longest eras of human history. And they still exist worldwide.[52]

In This Chapter ...

The economic fallout from the coronavirus pandemic in (so-called) Australia,[53] has mirrored that of other countries of the Global North: a 'pandeconomy' that has both illuminated and compounded the social, economic and environmental polycrises taking place through 'the intensification of capitalism throughout the world.'[54] The very real costs of the pandemic continue. Unemployment, homelessness and financial insecurity affect all genders, yet the pandemic continues to impact upon women in particular ways; ways linked with caregiving.

In the Next Chapter ...

As the pandemic develops, the social, economic and *caregiving crises* of twenty-first century capitalism are compounded. In the findings of *Generation Expendable?*—a study exploring women's labour at the pandemic frontline—we see the businesses of caring characterised by poor virus protections, insecure work, and a strikingly high incidence of workplace bullying.

Notes

1. Kerschner, C., Wächter, P., Nierling, L., & Ehlers, M. H. (2018). Degrowth and Technology: Towards feasible, viable, appropriate and convivial imaginaries. Journal of cleaner production, 197, 1619–1636.
2. Bhar, S. (2020). Degrowth and COVID-19: Are we drawing a simplistic connection? Mongabay, April 21, 2020. https://india.mongabay.com/2020/04/commentary-degrowth-and-covid-19-are-we-drawing-a-simplistic-connection/. Accessed July 2021.
3. Cannon, S. (2019). Climate strikes: Greta Thunberg calls for 'system change not climate change' – here's what that could look like. The Conversation, Mar 15, 2019. Also see: Systems Change not Climate Change. https://systemchangenotclimatechange.org/.
4. Wray, M. (2020). Dolphins return to Italy's coast amid coronavirus lockdown: 'Nature just hit the reset button'. Global News, Mar 18, 2020. https://globalnews.ca/news/6697281/dolphins-italy-coronavirus/.
5. Savini, F. (2021). Towards an urban degrowth: Habitability, finity and polycentric autonomism. Environment and Planning A: Economy and Space, 53(5), 1076–1095.
6. The Standard. (2020). Elephants 'get drunk on corn wine and fall asleep after breaking into Chinese village' story debunked. https://www.standard.co.uk/news/world/elephants-break-into-chinese-village-get-drunk-corn-wine-a4392301.html. Accessed July 2021.
7. Dapcevich, M. (2020). Multiple Cougars Seen Wandering the Streets of Santiago Amid Coronavirus Lockdown. EcoWatch April 9, 2020. https://www.ecowatch.com/cougar-santiago-coronavirus-2645673513.html. Accessed July 2021.
8. Reuters. (2020). Chilean capital gets another visit from cougar amid coronavirus lockdown. https://www.reuters.com/article/us-health-coronavirus-chile-puma-idUSKBN21K37Q. Accessed July 2021.
9. Telep. P. (2020). Some Don't Realize What a Profound Gift of Time This Pandemic Is. UCF News, July 29, 2020. https://www.ucf.edu/news/some-dont-realize-what-a-profound-gift-of-time-this-pandemic-is/. Accessed July 2021.
10. In 2023 the number of signatories is now above 2000.
11. The Open Letter Working Group, Degrowth.info (2020). *Degrowth.info Blog*, May 5, 2020. https://degrowth.info/blog/more-than-1000-experts-call-for-degrowth-as-post-covid-19-path.

12. Degrowth.info Blog. (2020). Re-imagining the Future After the Corona Crisis. https://degrowth.info/en/open-letter. Accessed May 2021.
13. Sutcliff, H. (2020). COVID-19: The 4 building blocks of the Great Reset. World Economic Forum, Aug 11, 2020. https://www.weforum.org/agenda/2020/08/building-blocks-of-the-great-reset/ Accessed Nov 2020.
14. Leff, E. (2018). Degrowth or deconstruction of the economy- Towards a sustainable world. *Contours of Climate Justice. Ideas for shaping new climate and energy politics*, pp. 101–107. Aug 8, 2018.
15. Liegey, V., & Nelson, A. (2020). Cited in Degrowth is a Radical Solution to the Climate Crisis. *HuckMag*, Sept 22, 2020. https://www.huckmag.com/article/degrowth-is-a-radical-solution-to-the-climate-crisis. Accessed July 2021.
16. da Silva, G. (2020). COVID-19 Drop in Pollution to be Short-lived. Pursuit, University of Melbourne. March 30, 2020, https://pursuit.unimelb.edu.au/articles/covid-19-drop-in-pollution-to-be-short-lived. Accessed July 2022.
17. Paulsen, S. (2020). Degrowth and feminisms ally to forge care-full paths beyond pandemic. *Interface: A journal for and about social movements.* Movement report, Volume 12 (1): 232–246 (July 2020), p. 235.
18. Price, J. (2020). The endless urging of Victoria to open up is baffling. Sydney Morning Herald, Sept 8, 2020. https://www.smh.com.au/national/the-endless-urging-of-victoria-to-open-up-is-baffling-20200906-p55swi.html. Accessed July 2021.
19. Markham, F., & Smith, D. (2020). Indigenous Australians and the COVID 19 crisis: perspectives on public policy. P. 2.
20. Le Grand, C., and Powell, D. (2020). Melbourne a 'Petri dish' for retail disruption. The Age, Aug 3, 2020. https://www.theage.com.au/national/victoria/melbourne-a-petri-dish-for-retail-disruption-20200803-p55i5x.html. Accessed July 2021.
21. Platinum. (2022). Melbourne Lockdown Dates 2020, 2021 and 2022. https://www.platinumaccounting.com.au/melbourne-lockdown-dates/. Accessed March 2023.
22. ABC Factcheck. (2021). Is Melbourne the Most Locked Down City in the World? https://www.abc.net.au/news/2021-10-25/fact-check-is-melbourne-most-locked-down-city/100560172. Accessed March 2023.
23. Australian Institute of Health and Welfare (AIHW). (June 2021). Young Australians highly impacted by COVID-19. https://www.aihw.gov.au/news-media/media-releases/2021-1/june/young-australians-highly-impacted-by-covid-19. Accessed Dec 2022.
24. Kabatek, J. (2020). How COVID-19 is Hitting Australia's Young Adults Hard. The Conversation, Oct 7, 2020. https://theconversation.com/5-charts-on-how-covid-19-is-hitting-australias-young-adults-hard-147254. Accessed Dec 2022.

25. Boyle, J., Garad, R. and Teede, H. (2020.) There's a fundamental need to reverse the 'pink recession. Dec 14, 2020. https://lens.monash.edu/@medicine-health/2020/12/14/1381848/theres-a-fundamental-need-to-reverse-the-pink-recession. Accessed Jan 2021.
26. Boyle et al. (2020). Ibid.
27. McKinsey & Company. (2020). The pandemic's gender effect. Quarterly Fifty Five. https://www.mckinsey.com/featured-insights/diversity-and-inclusion/five-fifty-the-pandemics-gender-effect. Accessed Dec 2020.
28. Australian Bureau of Statistics. (2023, updated). Labour Force Australia. https://www.abs.gov.au/statistics/labour/employment-and-unemployment/labour-force-australia/latest-release. Accessed June 2021.
29. The Australian Institute of Criminology reports that the pandemic brought an increase in frequency and severity of physical and sexual violence for women, and of coercive control. Two-thirds of women who had experienced partner violence prior to COVID said the violence had escalated. More than half of women reported escalation of emotionally abusive, harassing or controlling behaviours during the pandemic.
30. Boxall, H. Morgan, A. & Brown R. (2020). The prevalence of domestic violence among women during the COVID-19 pandemic. Statistical Bulletin no. 28. Canberra: Australian Institute of Criminology. https://doi.org/10.52922/sb04718.
31. Alon, T., Coskun, S., Doepke, M., Koll, D., & Tertilt, M. (2021). From Mancession to Shecession: Women&Apos; S employment in regular and pandemic recessions.
32. Wallace, C. (2020). Victory, history and a pink recession: The highs and lows for women in 2020.
33. Australian Bureau of Statistics. (2022). National Study of Mental Health and Wellbeing. Reference period. 2020–21. https://www.abs.gov.au/statistics/health/mental-health/national-study-mental-health-and-wellbeing/latest-release. Accessed Nov 2022.
34. Risse, L. (2020). Undervalued and unseen: Australia's COVID-19 frontline workforce. The Power to Persuade. Apr 14, 2020. https://www.powertopersuade.org.au/blog/undervalued-and-unseen-australias-covid-19-frontline-workforce/14/4/2020. Accessed June 2020.
35. Froud, J., Haslam, C., Johal, S. and Williams, K. (2020). (How) does productivity matter in the foundational economy? Local Economy, 35(4), pp. 316–336. https://journals.sagepub.com/doi/pdf/10.1177/0269094220956952. Accessed Nov 2022.
36. Bentham, J., Bowman, A., de la Cuesta, M., Engelen, E., Ertürk, I., Folkman, P., & Williams, K. (2013). Manifesto for the foundational economy. *Manchester: Centre for Research on Socio-Cultural* Change.

37. Lewis, T. Holcombe-James, I., & Glover, A. (2022). More than just 'working from home': domestic space, economies and living infrastructures during and beyond pandemic times. Cultural Studies, 1–23. https://doi.org/10.1080/09502386.2022.2142804.
38. Green, F. J., & O'Reilly, A. (Eds.). (2021). *Mothers, mothering, and COVID-19: Dispatches from the pandemic.* Demeter Press.
39. Riach, K., O'Hare, C., Dalton, B., & Wang, C. (2018). The Future Face of Poverty is Female: Stories Behind Australian Women's Superannuation Poverty in Retirement.
40. Senate Economics References Committee. (2016). 'A husband is not a retirement plan': Achieving economic security for women in retirement. Parliament of Australia.
41. Australians Investing in Women. (2021) Changing the Trajectory: Investing in Women for a Fairer Future, Equity Economics, November 2021. https://static1.squarespace.com/static/61b14c4abbc81a1543f55180/t/621876d781781b3b2f8e4633/1645770486120/EE_Women_Fairer%2BFuture_WEB_SPREADS.pdf Accessed Jan 2023.
42. Antrobus, P. (2004). Audio recording from conference The Gift Economy inside and outside Patriarchal Capitalism: A Radically Different Worldview is Possible. http://gift-economy.com/the-gift-economy-inside-and-outside-patriarchal-capitalism-part-4/. Accessed December 2022.
43. Risse, L. (2020). Undervalued and unseen: Australia's COVID-19 frontline workforce. Power To Persuade, April 14, 2020. https://www.powertopersuade.org.au/blog/undervalued-and-unseen-australias-covid-19-frontline-workforce/14/4/2020.
44. Commisceo Global. (Undated). Australia - Culture, Etiquette and Business Practices. https://www.commisceo-global.com/resources/country-guides/australia-guide. Accessed Jan 2023.
45. Rule of Law Education, (Undated). https://www.ruleoflaw.org.au/eureka-rebellion/democracy-timeline/. Accessed July 2022.
46. Workpoints Play Blog. (Undated). 25 company values from Australia's best workplaces. https://www.workpointsplay.com/blog/2021/25-company-values. (Accessed May 2023).
47. Feminisms and Degrowth Alliance. (2020). Feminist degrowth reflections on COVID-19 and the politics of social reproduction. Degrowth Blog, April 14, 2020. https://degrowth.info/blog/feminist-degrowth-collaborative-fada-reflections-on-the-covid-19-pandemic-and-the-politics-of-social-reproduction. Accessed July 2022.
48. Throsby, D. (2001). *Economics and culture.* Cambridge University Press. p. 6.
49. Shadmi, E. (2011). Meaning is a feminist Issue. Women's Worlds, Ottawa, July 7, 2011. http://gift-economy.com/erella-shadmi-meaning-is-a-feminist-issue/.

50. Commons Network. (2021). Living Well on a Finite Planet: Building a caring world beyond growth. A Commons Network Publication. p. 4.
51. Savini, F. (2021). Towards an urban degrowth: Habitability, finity and polycentric autonomism. Environment and Planning A: Economy and Space, 53(5), 1076–1095. https://doi.org/10.1177/0308518X20981391.
52. Goettner-Abendroth, H. (2004). Matriarchal Society: Definition and Theory. Published in The Gift, A Feminist Analysis. Athanor Books, Meltemi (Eds). Rome. (2004). Accessed July 2022.
53. The continent/country now called Australia was first 'founded' by the Dutch, and then invaded and 'settled' by the British. The lands were never ceded, and no treaty was ever agreed with First Nations peoples. This book is therefore, written and read on lands that always were, and always will be, Aboriginal lands.
54. Antrobus, P. (2004). The Gift Economy inside and outside Patriarchal Capitalism: A Radically Different Worldview is Possible, Part 4. Audio recording: http://gift-economy.com/the-gift-economy-inside-and-outside-patriarchal-capitalism-part-4/. Accessed July 2022.

CHAPTER 2

Generation Expendable?

Abstract The onset of the coronavirus sharply impacted Australian workers and workplaces. For women over 40, many staffing the 'care frontline', the conditions of work brought increased exposure to risk, including psychological harms as a result of bullying workplace cultures. With Australia's 'retirement incomes system' assuming a breadwinner model of full-time work across 40+ years, and zero housing costs in retirement, the author details the findings of her *Generation Expendable?* study, a snapshot of changes to women's work circumstances, conditions, and workplace relationships under COVID; considering whether 'older' women workers were framed as more 'expendable' in the early months of the pandemic as a result of their susceptibility to the 'dual discriminations' of ageism and sexism. Having foreseen that conditions at work would likely deteriorate during the crisis, that over half of women surveyed cited experiences of inappropriate and/or bullying workplace behaviours was shocking. That much of this bullying came from female colleagues even more so.

Keywords Care • Women • Labour • Healthcare • Education • Pandemic • COVID • Ageism • Sexism • Dual discriminations • Gendered ageing

M. Jordan, *Women's Work in the Pandemic Economy*,
https://doi.org/10.1007/978-3-031-40154-1_2

Introduction

This chapter describes the findings of *Generation Expendable?* a 'snapshot' study of the economic 'fallout' of the pandemic upon women workers aged over 40. The aim of *Generation Expendable?* was to record changes to women's work circumstances, conditions and workplace cultures 'under COVID'; including the degree to which these had been affected by pandemic 'stressors'. The survey incorporated both open and closed questions. All participants were invited to participate in a paid interview. In total, the survey gained 514 views, 329 starts and 152 completed responses. There were eleven interviews. All case studies and quotes are anonymised.

Changes to Circumstances

Around three quarters of the women surveyed (72.4%), had experienced 'changes to work circumstances or conditions' as a result of the pandemic. At the time of their completing the questionnaire, 85% had, however, either retained or regained employment.

Reasons for these higher retention rates than seen with younger workers seemed to be twofold: Firstly, a good number of survey respondents were employees of now 'essential' industries, principally, staffing the care frontline.

Additionally, it was evident that their longevity in the labour market meant that a high proportion this group of women were fortunate in being securely tenured. Overall, 42.8% of women workers reported being contracted in permanent and full-time jobs. A further 19.7% cited permanent part-time work.[1] Around 12.5% of women surveyed stated they were working 'casual or short-term contracts', and 5.3% 'fixed-term' contracts. Those remaining were either on the government furlough payment, 'JobKeeper', were 'self-employed', had taken 'early retirement' or self-described as 'unemployed and not seeking work'.

A few had secured a disability support pension or had become full-time students.[2,3]

Overall, around one fifth (19%) of older women had lost work as a direct result of the pandemic *at some point*, a notably better rate than that of younger workers.[4] Only around 14.5% described themselves as 'currently unemployed and seeking work':[5]

> I got let go as I was with the company for less than a year; four hours later I was offered two weeks' work. After two weeks sacked again. Next day offered an 8hr a fortnight contract. Worked 29hrs a week for four weeks. Offered a

45hr fortnight contract-worked 45hrs a week. After three months, the contract that was meant to be permanent reverts back to a casual contract.

Their unwillingness to make my position permanent prior [to COVID], meant that as soon as I needed to work from home they could fire me with no notice and no recourse. Was fired literally an hour after I requested to work from home.

Resilience to Change

Because the study had a focus on gendered ageing, the survey included questions relating to factors which might indicate women's 'financial resilience'. With Australian women over 50 one of the fastest-growing groups experiencing homelessness, and on average retiring with half the savings of Australian men, the data collected gave some indication of women workers' capacity to bounce back from the economic shocks of the crisis.[6,7]

These resilience factors included not only pecuniary, but 'identity' traits recognised as increasing (women's) vulnerability to 'structural' disadvantage. Categories included partner (income) status, Indigeneity, whether she spoke a language other than English at home, LGBTIQ+ identity, unpaid care responsibilities, disability and chronic health conditions: all circumstances well known to influence long-term financial security (see Fig. 2.1).[8,9,10,11]

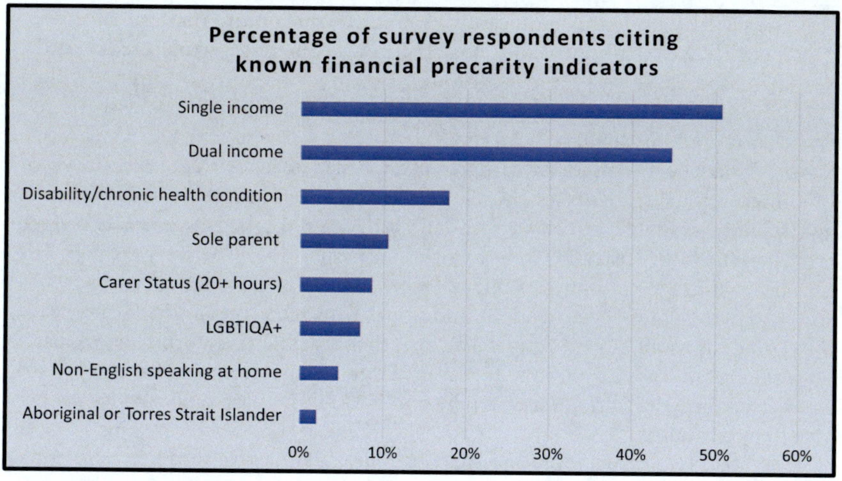

Fig. 2.1 Percentage of survey respondents citing known financial precarity indicators

Respondents housing status was also an indicator for financial resilience. With over half of women surveyed reliant on a single income, with one fifth 'sole mortgagees' and 20% 'private renters', it was of little surprise that 44.1% overall stated that 'negative financial impacts as a result of changes to work conditions or circumstances' arising from the crisis would affect their retirement.

With a retirement incomes system which assumes zero housing costs in older age and a breadwinner model (of full-time work across 40+ years of working life), Australian women are already structurally disadvantaged in typically having to balance family care work with paid employment.[12] Increased financial precarity arising from the pandemic would, for many women, mean the difference between a decent retirement and one marred by poverty.[13]

Changed Conditions of Work

Compared to their 'younger sisters', as noted above, the survey suggested that women over 40 had much healthier job security through greater likelihood of being permanently contracted and presumably more experienced in their chosen occupation, suggesting more transferable skills in a cool labour market.

This greater job security didn't, however, automatically translate into worker satisfaction, as the many survey comments detailed:

> Increased workload, significantly decreased autonomy, removal of equipment (e.g. telephone) and financial resources (e.g. work credit card), increased sense of precarity although no direct pressure on my individual job - but much on colleagues in very closely adjacent positions with a sense that it could easily have been me.
>
> I had been employed casually as an ESL[14] teacher to refugees and/or international students for over 9 years across different institutions. Work was steadily available but always casual. I haven't worked as a teacher since March 2020. Instead I found work as a casual postal delivery worker. It's bottom grade very physical menial work. Lucky to have it but …
>
> I was supposed to have an additional 6 months unpaid maternity leave (total 18 months paid & unpaid), and then be able to return to work part-time for at least 12 months. HR at my large organisation (5000+ employees) rejected my leave request and refuse to backfill my part-time role for longer than 6 months.
>
> I had two casual jobs, one as an exam invigilator at a university, the other interviewing for the Aged Care Royal Commission. I would have earned around $6000 annually for these 2 jobs, but in 2020 made a total of only around $1000.

Unsurprisingly, the survey identified that around 40% of the women had been asked, or had requested, to work from home, making this the most common 'change to work circumstances'. For some it was a positive experience, offering improved work/life balance and greater autonomy in the job.

For others however, the unexpected and often involuntary change saw them foundering:

> Working from home with little to no support, no plan in place for the well-being of staff. The working situation changed but the workplace made no new support plans.
>
> I chose to work from home which I thought was going to be a month or so. Then came suggestions that we needed to employ younger people who were healthy and less likely to need to work from home. I was a female, over 60, with a chronic disease and ostracized for working from home. They said it was my choice. I emphasized that it was a government and CEO directive. I have worked my whole life, with 2 children since I was 15 years and 3 months old. I now feel worthless.

As with younger women, working in the home also brought some older women into proximity to danger:

> I was renting with my de-facto husband in New South Wales. The pandemic made his controlling behaviour much worse and badly impacted my mental health. I tried to commit suicide. After 3 weeks in hospital, I packed everything up and moved to Melbourne where I rent a flat with one of my sons. Relocating was supported by my employer. [But] because I needed time off due to a mental health crisis, I feel I am considered a liability.[15,16]

The Education Frontline

As noted above, a significant number of *Generation Expendable?* respondents had identified as working in the newly essential industries of the COVID frontline. Chiefly, the female-dominated sectors of education, healthcare, aged-care and community services.[17]

From the early days of the pandemic, the potential closure of schools had been the subject of intense public debate in Naarm, where economic lockdowns were first implemented.[18] Arguments centered on the importance of supervising children so that their parents could 'keep the economy running'.[19] But there were also deliberations on the importance of a school routine and social connection for young people; how to balance these factors against virus risk and mental health considerations. While such discussions were important, the wellbeing of school workers, not only teachers, but teaching assistants, clerical staff, school cleaners and more, was notably absent.[20]

As a sector boasting a three-quarters' female staff, with a majority aged over 40, the tenor of the public debate begged questions around how these older women workers were valued, implying at best a certain 'invisibility', and at worse, an implicit *expendability* of this older labour cohort.[21,22,23]

Certainly, many female school staff felt abandoned:

> We were expected to continue attending school with little to no consideration given to our personal circumstances, risks to family members. We were expected to educate the children attending school, ensure they socially distanced (impossible with young children), clean and clean and clean with no training or PPE [personal protective equipment]. Our workload tripled overnight.
>
> I didn't feel safe working in overcrowded schools where students and teachers rush through a small space and students were 'joke-coughing' at teachers.
>
> I worked as a casual relief teacher prior to the pandemic, then, because of my age, I felt it dangerous to be working as schools were advising teachers over 60 to retire or take leave.
>
> Some schools offered 55+ the option to work from home, my school didn't.

Healthcare Services

Employers and policymakers were also slow in protecting the feminised healthcare workforce. In the state of Victoria, the rollout of PPE was sluggish, with uniforms often unfit for (smaller build) women workers.[24] For nurses, almost 90% of whom are women and 48% aged over 45, the pressures of managing the sick and the 'health vulnerable', alongside their own anxieties, were immense.[25,26]

Added to what initially were somewhat lax safety protocols, women were routinely working in poorly ventilated and enclosed environments, something which was particularly distressing for aged- and community-care workers, who routinely needed to engage in intimate contact with their vulnerable clientele:

> I was not considered to be in a high-risk group, so was expected to continue to work face to face in a workplace with around 1000 people. This seemed surreal.

Chronically understaffed and heavily reliant on casual/agency labour, occupational health and safety (OH&S) risk in residential care settings increased sharply under COVID.[27] Already a sector known for the 'neglect and abuse' of residents, aged care facilities faced the same, extreme challenges that had been flagged weeks earlier in other countries, with a growing sense of despair:[28]

> Lost confidence in the workplace.
>
> Less oversight in the Aged Care Facility. Management were aware spot checks could not occur during Covid. Decreasing staff numbers, bullying, harassment and financial threats to staff. Minimal resources, ordering not complete. Resident care has suffered. Staff morale has suffered. This continues.
>
> Management have taken staff off the floor to attend to paperwork. Understaffing is rife, staff are burnt out and in distress. Residents are in distress. Our [aged care] site is female-dominated and we have been bullied and manipulated, threatened with financial ramifications. I have spoken out and am being targeted for doing so.

Worker Agency

Under normal labour market conditions, women workers in the business of care' might have sought new jobs or taken action through their union. Indeed, *Generation Expendable?* revealed that over half of women *had* in fact 'raised issues directly' with workplace decision-makers, to 'challenge decisions, processes or behaviours in relation to pandemic workplace changes'.

It was testament to female agency under treacherous circumstances. Rating the success of these actions however, survey respondents reported on average a measly 4.3 out of 10, with almost one quarter of workers (24.7%) seeing 'no resolution at all'.[29,30]

With the job 'market' stalled, women had little recourse but to accept deteriorating conditions at work. This decline seemed to resonate across the board, but most typically, at the care frontline, where a sharp increase in workload came from newly imposed and often onerous tasks of cleaning and sanitisation, the monitoring of physical distancing mandates, and other COVID mitigation measures.

Survey respondents frequently described chaotic conditions of work:

> The pressure on us to perform fulltime plus evenings … the screaming and shouting and BLAMING was too stressful, and I resigned. My nerves are shot. I was on Job Seeker and took a 20 percent pay cut in an already underpaid industry.

The Dual Discriminations

With a key hypothesis of the research being to test whether 'older' women were something of an expendable worker cohort during COVID; their combined age and gender resulting in 'dual discrimination', was definitely a factor seen to be driving poor outcomes at work for some women:[31,32]

> Male dominated industry – no men lost their jobs in my department.

Overall, one in three women surveyed, (32.2%), believed the combination of their age and female gender had shaped their workplace outcomes and experiences during the pandemic, with 28.3% stating that they believed that their being female 'may have influenced decisions made or proposed' in relation to their employment.

Age discrimination was also cited as an adverse factor for a quarter (24.3%) of participants; particularly those seeking reemployment:

> NONE of the jobs I have applied for have resulted in calls from prospective employers nor interviews despite my having experience.
>
> The industry seems to be chasing younger workers with less experience. More pliable and able to be trained in the way the company wants…a very male dominated workforce…
>
> Mostly hospitality jobs and physical jobs like fruit picking in heat available, but given my age and health I cannot attempt long hours in these areas.
>
> I work in accounts and when I apply for a job, my resume works, I get an interview. However when my prospective employer sees me I am automatically dropped off the list. Most times I can see it in the interviewer's or receptionist's face. As I need my Centrelink payment, I have to apply for jobs each month with no expectation of getting any of them. I do have a small job of 4 hours per week which I got through one of my old bosses and am grateful to have that.

Relationships and Workplace Culture

Having anticipated that the circumstances and conditions of women's employment would inevitably have been affected by the crisis, responses to the third research theme relating to any impacts of the crisis upon work behaviours, relationships and work culture hadn't been forecast.

That acute pandemic 'stressors', both internal and external to the workplace would inevitably strain worker relationships, meant that it was pleasing to note some positive and collegial experiences recounted by study participants (see Fig. 2.2).

More commonly however, survey respondents and interviewees described practices and work cultures conspicuous for almost routine demonstrations of inappropriate workplace behaviour and shockingly high rates of what could be classified as workplace bullying.

Occasionally, relationship challenges were well managed:

> Management were supportive and assisted me to deal with an aggressive co-worker. I believe that the aggressive behaviour was directly linked to the co-worker struggling to cope with increased workload and stress-related.

Ellie's Story:

Ellie had only recently passed her probationary period at XXXX University when COVID hit. Although she had been working in a supportive team of ten, the pandemic triggered Ellie's pre-existing PTSD and major depressive disorder. Staff had initially been offered voluntary redundancy or early retirement and although this was later taken off the table, it left Ellie anxious about her job security. After seeking advice from her team leader, Ellie opted to take reduced hours and extra (purchased) leave. Describing herself as an "introvert", Ellie would like to remain working from home, as she has found it easier and appreciates being able to undertake household tasks while still doing her paid role. Ellie described "feeling privileged" in comparison to many other workers.

Fig. 2.2 Case study: Ellie, university librarian. (Ellie's story was published previously in *Generation Expendable? Older women in the pandeconomy.* (Feb 2022). See: www.grassrootsresearch.com.au.)

More frequently however, the pandemic workplace was described as 'toxic'. A whopping *58.6%* of women workers 'didn't feel supported by management', and either 'disagreed' (30.9%) or 'weren't sure' (25.7%), even whether 'established policies and procedures were adhered to'.

Frequently, women described workplace relations buckling under pressure:

> I changed jobs due to a toxic and bullying work environment. I had been forced to take a 20 percent pay cut with no reduction in hours.
>
> It was a very humiliating time, it broke me: counsellor, 6 weeks off work … When I returned, I was removed from my role and changed work-site, some co-workers refused to engage with me. Still too emotionally affected to talk about my experience.

Psychological Harms at Work

The commonality of lapsed standards at work was seen in almost one third of women (30.1%), reporting an 'impact on workplace health and safety' under COVID.

To canvas the nature of pandemic impacts on workplace culture, that is, *psychological* health and safety risks, workers were invited to list their experiences of 'inappropriate workplace behaviours' which, if ongoing in nature, are recognised by Australia's Fair Work Commission as constituting workplace bullying (see Fig. 2.3).

Under Australian law, workplace bullying is only indictable if the activities are ongoing and also result in a negative impact upon a worker.[33] For example, a worker might make repeated jokes about a colleague's accent, but if the target isn't negatively impacted it does not legally constitute workplace bullying.

That women working the COVID 'care frontline' were experiencing tremendous *psychological* pressures was shown in the shockingly high incidence of inappropriate workplace behaviours recorded by the *Generation Expendable?* survey. In a second question exploring work cultures during COVID, participants were shown a more nuanced list of bullying behaviours taken from a study of bullying in the UK's National Health Service (NHS).[34] Here, 52.4% of Australian women related work conditions and work relationships which aligned with the NHS research definitions (see Fig. 2.4).[35]

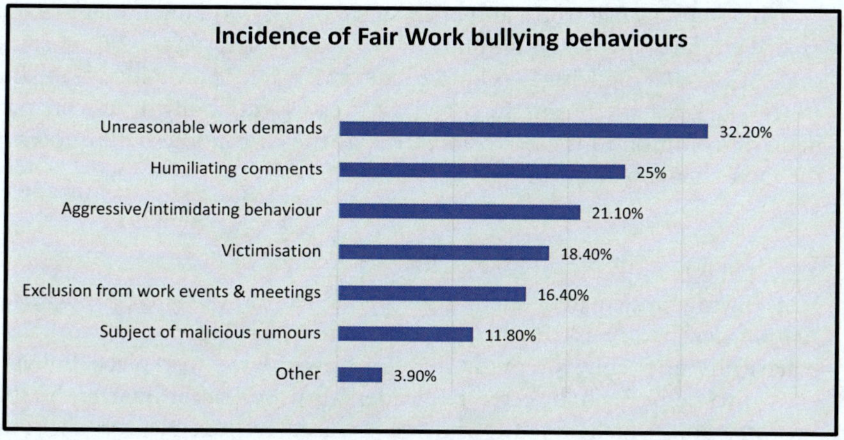

Fig. 2.3 Incidence of bullying behaviours as defined under Australian Fair Work legislation

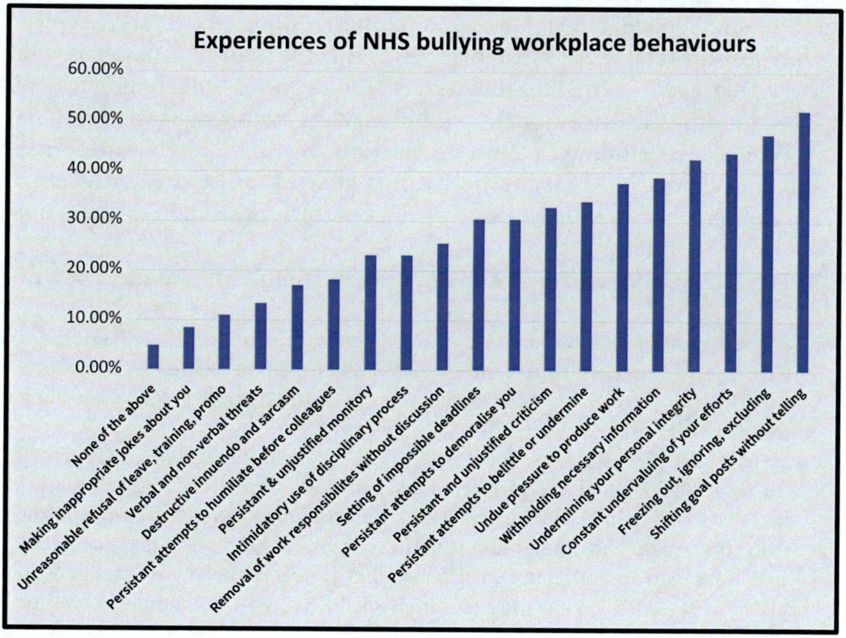

Fig. 2.4 Recorded incidence of bullying behaviours as defined in NHS Study, UK, 2013

While only a small study, and of a specific cohort working under extraordinary circumstances, the findings of *Generation Expendable?* were stark; suggesting that bullying workplace cultures weren't an abberation, but were in fact *normal* during the coronavirus crisis, with bullying at work particularly common in the care industries, as the case studies and quotes in the next chapters illustrate.

What Wasn't Asked

Not having anticipated such high incidence of bullying, *Generation Expendable?* hadn't asked who the perpetrators of inappropriate workplace behaviours and cultures might be. However, with workplace bullying known to be typically directed by 'leaders' towards subordinates, the survey question which asked, 'who was mainly responsible for decision-making in relation to your job?', gave some indication of which workers were targeted and by whom within the workplace hierarchy.[36,37]

A majority of respondents (45.4%) had, unsurprisingly, cited a male leader or leaders, as responsible for the decisions which impacted their job. However, female leaders came a close second, at 40.1%. Typically, 'decision-makers' were aged over 40, reflecting cultural patterns which show that even in the feminised sectors, older men still dominate senior roles, leaving the operational 'middle' management tier to women.[38,39,40]

While not claiming a robust correlation, if the link between decision-making powers and bullying behaviours at work was correct, *Generation Expendable?* had revealed a quite distinct pattern of women workers bullying other women.

It was a trend confirmed in many survey comments and interviews:

> It speaks volumes about a world in which women turn on other women; no better than the men we try and escape. Fickle woman leading in her man's world. Why we feel we need to become [a man] in order to live amongst them, I will never understand.
>
> My boss picked on me prior to COVID – even putting me in Coventry for six months but that's another story. I always felt disliked and resented. I had disclosed being neurodiverse and she certainly targeted my communication style – or what she saw as a lack thereof. She shared false (and confidential) information about me with colleagues too. The behaviour ramped up under COVID. I was already routinely excluded, and my input ignored or mocked, but one final email attack – I walked the streets for two hours so my kids couldn't witness me crying. With advice from my union, I lodged a

staff grievance. I considered it an internal matter so was pretty shocked when she involved the Board and threatened legal action. I'd kept records though. The Board agreed a substantial payout – but I had to sign an NDA.[41] As an organisation advocating for workers' rights – including for older women – it was terrible. I'm still on medication for both my physical and mental health. In my new job they celebrate difference.

We have a new boss who has employed her friends-making herself a support team, and she has treated the rest of the team as expendable. She refused my request for long service leave even though I gave her 5 1/2 months' notice to cover only 4 shifts. I am more skilled in patient care than she is and I suspect she resents this.

In This Chapter …

The onset of the coronavirus sharply impacted Australian workers and workplaces, as it had in other countries. For women, many staffing the care frontline, the conditions of work brought increased risk on all fronts, not least in lapsed OH&S standards, exposure to bullying workplace cultures and related psychological hazards.

In the Next Chapter …

With *Generation Expendable?* exposing extreme levels of workplace bullying, I consider whether this behaviour is 'pandemic' or 'endemic' in nature. Might the study have revealed something inherent to the way that Australians work?, Something about our national culture? In the next chapter I explore potential drivers for bullying and related exclusions which structure the labour market and deem 'women's work' as less valuable—still.[42]

Notes

1. Although not a direct survey question, the qualitative data gathered from open questions and from interviews showed that many workers came from the 'frontline' sectors of education and healthcare. The survey was shared on Twitter by a well-known education and gender advocate. With over half of total responses coming through on that day, this likely explains the high rates of respondents from the education and health sectors.
2. ABS figures rely on 'jobseekers' receiving Centrelink payments, and therefore do not capture statistics relating to underemployment, or to women who may be 'multiployed' in low-paying jobs.

3. Taylor, D. (2021). Women were let go in greater numbers during COVID, now they face being offered lower-paid roles to return to work. Australian Broadcasting Corporation News. Feb 12, 2021. https://www.abc.net.au/news/2021-02 12/women-with-degrees-lost-jobs-in-greater-numbers-than-men-covid/13146120. Accessed Jan 2023.
4. 'Fixed-term contracts' could be either short term or longer term.
5. Respondents were able to select more than one answer. For example, women might be both casually employed and registered unemployed and thus 'jobseeking'.
6. McFerran, L. (2010). It could be you: Female, single, older and homeless. *Parity*, *23*(10), 15–18.
7. Petersen, M., & Parsell, C. (2014). Older women's pathways out of homelessness in Australia.
8. Jordan, M. (2022). Gendered Housing. New Economy Journal, October 2022. https://www.neweconomy.org.au/journal/issues/vol3/october-2022/gendered-housing/.
9. Clare, R. (2017). Cited by WGEA at https://www.wgea.gov.au/publications/superannuation-gender-pay-gaps-by-age-group. Accessed Jan 2023.
10. Whitson, R. (2021). How much money do you need to retire? The answer depends on one big thing. Australian Broadcasting Corporation News online, June 15, 2021. https://www.abc.net.au/news/2021-06-15/retirement-superannuation-super-money-investment-home-ownership/100208500. Accessed Jan 2023.
11. Giroir, G. (2020). How Men and Women Spend Their Money Differently. Louisiana Federal Credit Union. https://www.louisianafcu.org/articles/how-men-and-women-spend-their-money-differently. Accessed Jan 2023.
12. Warwick, S. (2016). The Adequacy of the Age Pension. Per Capita Australia.
13. Fawkner, D., & Lester, L. (2020). 400,000 women over 45 are at risk of homelessness in Australia. *The Conversation*, August 2020. https://theconversation.com/400-000-women-over-45-are-at-risk-of-homelessness-in-australia-142906. Accessed Nov 2021.
14. 'ESL' refers to teaching 'English as a second language'.
15. The Australian Institute of Criminology report suggests there was a significant underreporting of family violence during the pandemic.
16. Australian Institute of Health and Welfare. (Dec 2021) Family, domestic and sexual violence service responses in the time of COVID-19. https://www.aihw.gov.au/getmedia/9d808ec3-8c3a-452d-b435-b0afa1df866d/aihw-fdv-8.pdf.aspx?inline=true. Accessed Jan 2023.
17. OECD Library. (2010). Economic sectors with the highest feminisation rates are health and community services followed by education. Female employment in service activities in OECD countries, 2010. https://doi.org/10.1787/9789264179370-en. Accessed Jan 2023.

18. National Excellence in School Leadership Initiative (NESLI). (2018). Nearly one in two teachers undergo discrimination in their school. April 20, 2018. https://web.archive.org/web/20221126185106/http://wla.edu.au/yowsil-results.html. Accessed Feb 2023.
19. Australian Broadcasting Corporation. (2020). Why are schools still open in Australia? March 24, 2020. https://www.abc.net.au/news/2020-03-19/coronavirus-why-is-australia-keeping-schools-open/12070702. Accessed Dec 2022.
20. Billett, P.; Turner, K., & Xia Li. (2022). Australian teacher stress, well-being, self-efficacy, and safety during the COVID-19 pandemic, Psychology in the Schools, 09 May 2022. https://onlinelibrary.wiley.com/doi/10.1002/pits.22713. Accessed Jan 2023.
21. Australian Bureau of Statistics. (2018). 4125.0 – Gender Indicators, Australia, Sep 2018. https://www.abs.gov.au/ausstats/abs@.nsf/Lookup/by%20Subject/4125.0~Sep%202018~Main%20Features~Economic%20Security~4#:~:text=Employment%20and%20Labour%20force%20participation&text=The%20industries%20with%20the%20highest,industries%20(See%20Table%201.3).
22. Government of Australia, ANZSCO ID 2412 data on Primary School Teachers. Source: https://labourmarketinsights.gov.au/occupation-profile/primary-school-teachers?occupationCode=2412. Accessed Mar 2023.
23. McGrath, K. F., & Van Bergen, P. (2017). Are male teachers headed for extinction? The 50-year decline of male teachers in Australia. *Economics of Education Review*, 60, 159–167.
24. Anaesthesia, Journal of the Association of Anaesthetists. (2020). Personal protective respirator masks (PPE) often do not fit correctly, especially for women and Asian healthcare workers. Cited by CKN, Sept 16, 2020. https://www.ckn.org.au/content/personal-protective-respirator-masks-ppe-often-do-not-fit-correctly-especially-women-and. Accessed Nov 2020.
25. Australian College of Nursing. (2019). Healthy ageing in the nursing workforce. The Hive, July 22, 2019. https://www.acn.edu.au/the-hive-2019/healthy-ageing-nursing-workforce. Accessed Aug 2020.
26. Risse, L. (2020). Undervalued and unseen: Australia's COVID-19 frontline workforce. The Power to Persuade, April 14, 2020. http://www.powertopersuade.org.au/blog/undervalued-and-unseen-australias-covid-19-frontline-workforce/14/4/2020. Accessed Aug 2020.
27. Hodgkin, S., Warburton, J., Savy, P. & Warr, M. (2020). Workforce Crisis in Residential Aged Care: Insights from Rural, Older Workers. Australian Journal of Public Administration, vol. 76, no. 1, pp. 93–105. DOI:10.1111/1467-8500.12204. https://agedcare.royalcommission.gov.au/system/files/2020-06/RCD.9999.0256.0017.pdf. Accessed Aug 2020.

28. Royal Commission into Aged Care Quality and Safety. (2021). Summary of Final Report. https://agedcare.royalcommission.gov.au/sites/default/files/2021-03/final-report-executive-summary.pdf.
29. Nahum, D. & Stanford, J. (2020). 2020 year-end labour market review: insecure work and the COVID-19 pandemic. Centre for Future Work, The Australia Institute, Dec 30, 2020.
30. Javanparast, S., Freeman, T., Baum, F. et al. How institutional forces, ideas and actors shaped population health planning in Australian regional primary health care organisations. BMC Public Health 18, 383 (2018). https://doi.org/10.1186/s12889-018-5273-4.
31. Stypinska, J., & Turek, K. (2017). Hard and soft age discrimination: the dual nature of workplace discrimination. European Journal of Ageing, 14, 49–61.
32. Feldman, S. and Radermacher, H. (2016). Time of our lives?: building opportunity and capacity for the economic and social participation of older Australian women. Lord Mayor's Charitable Foundation (2016). At https://www.lmcf.org.au/images/2016-Time-of-Our-Lives-Report-LMCF.pdf.
33. Fair Work Commission (2023). https://www.fwc.gov.au/issues-we-help/bullying/what-bullying-work. Accessed Jan 2023.
34. As described on the Fair Work website in 2020. These have since been updated. See https://www.fwc.gov.au/issues-we-help/bullying/what-bullying-work.
35. Carter M, Thompson N, Crampton P., et al. (2013). Workplace bullying in the UK NHS: a questionnaire and interview study on prevalence, impact and barriers to reporting. BMJ Open 2013; 3:e002628. https://doi.org/10.1136/bmjopen-2013-002628.
36. Adams, A., Beasley, J., & Rayner, C. (1997). Bullying at work. Journal of Community and Applied Social Psychology, 7(3), 177–180. p. 2.
37. De Cieri, H., Sheehan, C., Donohue, R., Shea, T., & Cooper, B. (2019). Workplace bullying: an examination of power and perpetrators. Personnel Review.
38. Universal Class. Characteristics of Workplace Harassment Perpetrators. https://www.universalclass.com/articles/business/characteristics-of-workplace-harassment'perpetrators.htm. Accessed Jan 2023.
39. Yamada, D. (2008). Workplace Bullying and Ethical Leadership. The Journal of Values-based Leadership. Volume 1. Issue 2, article 5. p. 5.

    Citing US WBI/Zogby survey findings that '72 percent of bullies are bosses, and 55 percent of those bullied are rank-and-file workers' (WBI/Zogby, 2007, p. 1).

40. Only 12.5% reported decision-makers aged under 40. Around 19.1% reported leaders of 'mixed genders'; 13.8% of 'mixed ages'. No women reported a 'non-binary' decision-maker.
41. Non-Disclosure Agreement.
42. Doran, C. (2017). The Price of Prejudice: Women's Work and Labour Force Discrimination in Australian History. https://doi.org/10.4172/2332-0915.1000177. https://www.longdom.org/open-access/the-price-of-prejudice-womens-work-and-labour-force-discriminationin-australian-history-2332-0915-1000177.pdf. Accessed Aug 2020.

CHAPTER 3

The Toxic Workplace: For Women

Abstract *Generation Expendable?* had revealed significant lapses in workplace health and safety during COVID, including new psychological hazards. This chapter explores the extent to which workplace bullying was an issue for Australia prior to the coronavirus crisis, and if so, what broader cultural factors might be driving this. Through case studies, we see that women workers were not only often the targets of workplace bullying, but also *the perpetrators.* While extreme workload pressures may partly explain the 'toxic' workplace cultures of the pandemic, the author brings in external data to argue that bullying is in fact, the norm for many Australian workers, with highly competitive and hierarchical workplace cultures only reflecting now entrenched neoliberal tenets around economic 'growth', efficiency and profiteering. With the collective worker power typical of the 20th century now largely superseded by top-down decision-making, and with an increasingly casualised labour force, this chapter asks whether bullying behaviour has become a tacit workplace convention in Australia.

Keywords Workplace bullying • Mobbing • Pandemic • Culture • Australia • Neoliberalism

M. Jordan, *Women's Work in the Pandemic Economy*,
https://doi.org/10.1007/978-3-031-40154-1_3

Introduction

The NHS study referenced in the previous chapter, along with other research into workplace cultures, identifies 'perceived inequities in workload distribution' as a key driver of bullying—particularly in healthcare and education settings.[1,2,3,4,5,6,7,8]

With workload pressures growing sharply under COVID, it seemed likely that the extreme burden facing women employed in the businesses of caregiving might partly explain the bullying work cultures the study had uncovered. Indeed, 'increased workload' was cited by 38% of survey respondents.

While high workload levels undoubtedly constituted an OH&S threat during 2020 and 2021, the *Generation Expendable?* survey data also revealed that 'the toxic workplace' was the norm for many workers prior to COVID:[9]

> 'Proud to be profitable' mentality put patients and staff at risk as OH&S[10] were not adhered to and covid legislation breached constantly. Your hours and job were at risk if you complained or questioned …
>
> The pressure on us to perform fulltime plus evenings, resolving all the issues with residential strata … the screaming and shouting and blaming our industry [from clients] for cleaning etc. was too stressful. I took a 20% pay cut in an already underpaid industry and have resigned now and am not working. My nerves are shot.
>
> I recently resigned from my job due to bullying and heavy workload, even though I experienced negative financial impacts. I had started the year with a great job, then changed to a new job which was dreadful. The [female] director who I reported directly to showed no understanding of the work pressures and forced me to return to work as soon as we could. Workdays were 10+ hours. I experienced aggressive or intimidating behaviour, belittling or humiliating comments and differential treatment or 'victimisation'. I was 'the subject of malicious or unfair rumours', 'unreasonable work demands', 'persistent attempts to belittle' me and 'persistent and unjustified criticism.' I resigned because the workplace became unbearable.

A National Culture of Bullying?

While (perceived) workload inequities during COVID undoubtedly resulted in a decline in work conditions and relationships at work, research from the Australian Workplace Barometer had already flagged workplace bullying as a key issue for Australia well prior to 2020, noting in 2014 that

Australia rated sixth-highest of 36 Organization for Economic Cooperation and Development (OECD) countries for workplace bullying.[11,12,13]

Additional research by the employment regulator Safe Work Australia had found that the national average for workplace bullying had increased by *40%* between 2011 and 2015 alone. Similarly, a 2014 University of Wollongong paper based on self-reported mental health data suggested that, during their working lives, around 40% of Australians will experience bullying at work, with 32.6% 'bullied at least once a week'.[14,15]

Although known to be significantly underreported, Australia's Productivity Commission estimates the costs of workplace bullying to be between $6 billion and $36 billion *every year*.[16] Between 2016 and 2019, claims for harassment, bullying and occupational violence were made by female employees at over twice the rate of claims from male workers. Similarly, women workers' compensation claims relating to workload burden were almost twice the rates of those made by males.[17]

While bullying is typically 'top down', directed from someone in a leadership position towards a subordinate, it is a type of behaviour that also can come 'horizontally', from colleagues at a similar level of seniority engaging in a 'coordinated effort to undermine, shun, and exclude a worker considered a threat'. This 'mobbing', as it is characterised, was Margot's experience (see Fig. 3.1).[18,19]

Pandemic or Endemic?

The commonality of bullying experiences in *Generation Expendable?* begged questions around whether this was the result of pandemic conditions of work, or whether 'normal' Australian work culture was being reported.

Numerous comments suggested that bullying was endemic:

> No changes in my workplace can be attributed to the pandemic. [They] can only be attributed to perceptions that my age and gender make me less capable at work.
>
> My 2020 workplace has an absolutely toxic culture. This is long term and completely unrelated to Covid.
>
> The pandemic is irrelevant. Australian work culture is so screwed up … Bitching behind people's backs, bullying and intimidation. That is nothing to do with the pandemic. Because I am female and older, they literally act like a teenager who wants to go to a party and have a tantrum.
>
> I changed jobs due to a toxic and bullying work environment. I had been forced to take a 20% pay cut with no reduction in hours.

Margot's Story [3]

Prior to covid, I'd get asked, 'what's your future looking like? And I would just say 'I'm on a transition to retirement... three - five years'. I wasn't keen on hanging around unless I could contribute. They said that I should stay working. I was 65 and I'd had a second cancer diagnosis, but I took it on board, and everybody was supportive. I didn't get any sense they wanted me gone. When covid happened, everyone advised me to work from home because I was on chemo. I'm a chronic diseases nurse and had moved to this regional hospital 20 years before. I'd built up their Diabetes Centre and now supervised a team of 15 senior and junior staff. Mainly women around 40.

A few months in [to covid] I started hearing comments in zoom meetings. Things like, 'you don't really need to be working from home.' I increasingly got a sense nobody was interested in what I was saying. They were ignoring my direction and acting independently. Next I hear three of them have gone to the executive director to say they are unhappy with me working from home. So when I returned to onsite work, I instigated conflict resolution with an external facilitator. I had thought everything was going swimmingly but the issues continued. People were going one, two, even three levels above me - not to complain but to ask for something; or just to make comment on the roster: operational stuff I was responsible for.

One particular team member kept purposely questioning my authority; mistrusting my decision making. I had already been managing her behaviour as it cropped up. I'm not the sort of do things behind anybody's back. There are difficult people in every workplace and managing them can be problematic. I was seeking to understand her a little better. I had had to get onto her about time management a number of times. She would just say, 'We need more staff. We need more this and that'. I would say 'We just need to do things more efficiently.' In the business plan I was developing we were looking at more telehealth, remote consultations, etc.

After the initial complaint, I ran an issues log. In our weekly meetings I made sure to give everyone the opportunity to have their say because, you know, 'You're not communicating properly'. Apart from that old furphy, they couldn't name anything wrong. How can you work with that? If there's not a clear complaint, there's no clear resolution. There was still this push back though. A nurse I had mentored for five years started to turn against me and I don't know why - maybe she thought I'd be retired sooner? She'd been acting up in my position and she became very challenging, asking things like: 'I wasn't here last Wednesday, did you have a meeting?' And I'd reply; 'we have a meeting every Wednesday, you know that'. 'Yeah, well, I haven't seen the minutes'. 'The minutes are where they always are'. And I'd send an email confirming and reminding everybody 'this is where the minutes are filed.' This sort of conversation went on and on. At one stage I asked; 'Do you have a problem with me? You're questioning things and I just want to know if there's anything we should discuss?' She said no. I discussed it with my boss several times; what we were going to do, how we were going to resolve the conflict. I even wrote up a plan..

Fig. 3.1 Case study: Margot, the healthcare manager. (Margot's story was previously published in The Power to Persuade (September 8, 2022). See https://www.powertopersuade.org.au/blog/the-disability-educator-a-case-study-in-older-women-and-the-toxic-workplace/7/9/2022.)

The team had been collaborative and respectful initially, but in covid it just flipped a switch. The nurse who was acting as onsite manager when I was working from home decided to go to my boss about it. I think she felt that everything fell to her; she was overwhelmed. But when I asked her, 'What is it?' She just said, 'everything'. I'd say, 'What is everything? Drop some work in my lap' But she'd respond, 'everything we do is a problem. This isn't working well'. You couldn't pin her down. But if they can't come up with specifics... I can't mother teenagers... She decided to go to my boss and then they all decided to go: individually, not as a group. I think it's worse.

The issue was she felt I wasn't carrying my burden - in fact, she wasn't. When I was back on site, I remember one time I was preparing our annual planning meeting; putting the final touches on the new business plan and she came into my office and just said, 'You know this isn't working, don't you?' I said, "What? What's 'this?' 'It's just not working' she said. I turned my back and carried on.

A month later one of the team got another job. We had a collection; all signed a card. We were supposed to go for lunch, but lockdown meant we couldn't. The day she was leaving I went to her desk at midday and said, 'It's been great; you'll do well.' Encouraging stuff, you know. Then at 12:30, our normal meeting time, I went into the meeting room, and you know what? They were all there. There had been a presentation and everything and I wasn't invited. As soon as I walked in...the look of shock on their faces...

It was incredibly upsetting. I went upstairs and broke down. My manager was aware of everything because we'd been talking throughout and she said, 'just go home, go home.' And I haven't been back - I can't. I read my diary from over those months and can see it as plain as day how: the white anting, the gaslighting. All written down. Being ignored; questioned; overwritten. It was the very definition of workplace bullying because you can't pin them down. Each incident on its own is nothing, but when you hang them together, it tells a terrible story. I was getting treated for cancer but not one of them had said, 'Are you OK?' I had that little bit more to give, but kept hearing, 'We need to get some youngsters here. We need new blood.'

Fig. 3.1 (continued)

Workplace bullying is said to be 'one of the last forms of abuse where targets – men or women – are routinely disbelieved'. This was shown to be the case in *Generation Expendable?*, with a number of women reporting that they had experienced '*gaslighting*', with their lived experiences either disbelieved or dismissed, and even where they themselves were instead framed as 'the problem'. This was Rachel's experience (see Fig. 3.2).

Rachel's Story.[4]

I qualified as a teacher in my 40s and found I was particularly good with students with severe disabilities. It can be challenging, but I worked very well, I was passionate about it. I secured some contract work at a well-known school for challenging behaviours. I got on well with my colleagues, the pupils and their families. But one teacher...I knew intuitively this woman was competitive; blind to other people's needs. I was careful to placate her because I saw her bullying other staff. There's a sense that, 'Well it's not happening to me' and I feel guilty about that now, but the bully was a permanent staff member and the union rep. She was also best friends with the team leader and there was collusion.

When I would suggest something, she would routinely take credit. She would discourage me from doing extra training, saying, 'I'll teach you; I'll mentor you'. But that never happened. She used me for my ideas.

I was doing a good job and they offered me an ongoing position. I was grateful, but also felt all was not well. I was working 90 hours a week and holidays, while constantly navigating curve balls from this staff member. I was quite popular and when the Principal suggested that I could become a team leader too, that set the bully off. She started to micromanage me. I was separated from staff I had been working really well with and put into a new classroom. I was given the most students: ten kids with severe disabilities, when the Department [of Education] recommends maximum of four-six students. It meant 30 percent more administrative work; emotional work as well.

I was becoming intuitive to the dynamic of the place – the politics. In meetings, the bully would say things like: 'the teacher who has xxx student didn't do X and Y, isn't that terrible?' And it was my student. That started happening all the time; this dismissiveness and passive aggression. Initially, my reporting work had been hailed as thorough; now I was having to redo everything. I was really stressed about the spotlight on my work and complained a few times. But this just seemed to result in collusion by management. They were letting her run me.

One day the bully said to me, 'Can we talk?' and I thought, 'Fantastic, we can sort things out'. It turned out to be disciplinary meeting; about my 'difficulty in communicating'. I knew that I was articulate; that I actually showed her up when she made many mistakes. So I went to see the Principal and said, 'this has to stop'. The Principal agreed to mentor me for leadership and later said: 'I've asked her to back off'.

The next term, we were flat out. The emotional burden was enormous. The bully and her team leader friend ramped up the pressure on me, belittling me in meetings, changing support staff - I never knew what was happening. They even changed which students I taught for electives. They started timing my lunch breaks...

Fig. 3.2 Case study: Rachel, the disability educator. (Rachel's story was previously published in The Power to Persuade (September 8, 2022). See https://www.powertopersuade.org.au/blog/the-disability-educator-a-case-study-in-older-women-and-the-toxic-workplace/7/9/2022.)

watching me. And it wasn't only me, there were now groups of staff saying; 'why aren't management doing anything?'

One day I was left alone with a student with complex behavioural issues. All of a sudden, I was being mauled, bitten. He grabbed me by the mouth and pulled me to the ground, then ran off. I was in complete shock and called the nurse. The Principal came to the nursing station, and I said, 'we've had a really hard year. A lot of staff are unhappy. There's been complaints of bullying and yet nothing done yet'. And she just said, 'it's all gossip'. I was so angry. I didn't even receive proper first aid.

We have to record all incidents though, and it turned out this student was known to social welfare. His past included severe trauma. I was like a cat on a hot tin roof because of the incident. I had PTSD but just didn't realise. After work I would collapse in the car. I was traumatised; my fingers were bleeding from anxiety, and I was having panic attacks... bursting into tears at work. I would photograph injuries, holes in the wall. The other students were growing anxious too, but due to confidentiality, I wasn't able to tell other families what was going on: I was managing the situation alone.

I didn't take sick leave, because of the ongoing innuendoes about my capacity coming from the bullies, but I contacted the union and wrote to the Principal stating; 'this is having an impact on my wellbeing'.

From then on, the Principal micromanaged me. I was in her office three days times a day... responding to; 'Maybe you're not coping that well?' She offered no strategies to manage the violence. This was a work site! Then other staff started to look at me funnily; I was increasingly ignored in meetings; ostracised but at the same time being watched. I couldn't even sit in the staff room.

Things came to a head when the same student destroyed a changing cubicle. He tore off the toilet seat and taps, and we had to isolate him. I thought, 'this child is so traumatised'. I was called into the Principal's office, and she said, 'we're very concerned. You're clearly not coping' and I went 'what?!' I felt so powerless. I actually started to think, maybe you're right...maybe it is me... Yeah... gaslighting.

I went to the doctor straight away and was diagnosed with PTSD, depression and anxiety. I let the school know I was taking sick leave that very day and from there, was completely frozen out. They asked for my keys back, the iPad. Here I am suffering trauma and I was made to feel it was my fault. What's most heartbreaking is that the pupils suffered. Many staff resigned. Psychologically, it reverberates through your whole life. I thought that I wasn't good enough for teaching but in actual fact I was very good - that was the problem, the challenging of power. The workplace was never safe. Rules about 'top tier behaviours' weren't adhered to. There was no review of their processes; no checks or balances whatsoever. The bully has actually been promoted and is now in a senior position. This woman is not safe - let alone qualified. Teachers don't want to complain, they just move on.

Fig. 3.2 (continued)

Neoliberalism

Highly competitive and hierarchical work cultures are not unique to Australia. Rather, they are central to the neoliberal economic paradigm we see structuring work and social cultures the world over, through a discourse of 'growth', efficiency, productivity and profiteering that first emerged almost 50 years ago.[20,21,22]

With the collective worker power of twentieth century 'welfarism' superseded by top-down, or shareholder decision-making, and fortified by an increasingly precarious and casualised labour force, it is little wonder that 'the victimising behaviour of bullying is slowly, yet progressively, establishing itself as a tacit convention' in Australian workplaces.[23]

As Peggy Antrobus explains:

> In capitalism, the values of patriarchy – competition, hierarchy, domination – have been united with the values of the market … Making us concerned with equations, measurement, judgments of value, hierarchical categorizations, and quantifications of punishment and reprisal.[24]

The experiences of women workers in Australia's pandemic economy suggest workplace bullying is entrenched, even intrinsic to late-stage capitalism. It is also, as we shall see, partly a gendered and a racialised phenomenon, with the nation's colonial legacy still, I will argue, influencing the nation's institutions and labour market values.

In This Chapter …

Generation Expendable? had exposed serious lapses in OH&S during the early months of the coronavirus crisis, including significant psychological hazards arising from bullying workplace cultures for women workers. Already an issue preceding COVID, demanding work conditions in the businesses of care were undoubtedly exacerbated by the pandemic. Shockingly, not only were women the targets of workplace bullying, but often the perpetrators.

In the Next Chapter …

The pandemic places Australian women workers under new pressures, but what other factors might also be driving toxic work relationships? In the next chapter I will look at the broader cultural and macroeconomic conditions which shaped women's work both before and during the coronavirus crisis.

Notes

1. Carter, M., Thompson, N., Crampton, P., Morrow, G., Burford, B., Gray, C., & Illing, J. (2013). Workplace bullying in the UK NHS: a questionnaire and interview study on prevalence, impact and barriers to reporting. BMJ open, 3(6), e002628.
2. Baillien, E., De Cuyper, N. and De Witte, H., (2011). Job autonomy and workload as antecedents of workplace bullying: A two-wave test of Karasek's Job Demand Control Model for targets and perpetrators. Journal of occupational and Organizational Psychology, 84(1), pp. 191–208.
3. Quinlan, M. (2018). Why is workplace bullying so widespread and rising? Business Think. University of NSW. 16 January 2018. https://www.businessthink.unsw.edu.au/articles/why-is-workplace-bullying-so-widespread-and-rising. Accessed May 2020.
4. Trépanier,S.G.,Peterson,C.,Fernet,C.,Austin,S.andDesrumaux,P.(2021). When workload predicts exposure to bullying behaviours in nurses: The protective role of social support and job recognition. Journal of Advanced Nursing, 77(7), pp. 3093–3103.
5. Lamberth, B. B. (2015). Workplace Bullying in Healthcare: Part 3. *Radiology management*, *37*(3), 18–22.
6. Askew, D. A., Schluter, P. J., Dick, M. L., Régo, P. M., Turner, C., & Wilkinson, D. (2012). Bullying in the Australian medical workforce: cross-sectional data from an Australian e-Cohort study. *Australian health review*, *36*(2), 197–204.
7. Sharma, M. (2017). Workplace bullying: an exploratory study in Australian academia.
8. Riley, D., Duncan, D. J., & Edwards, J. S. (2009). Investigation of staff bullying in Australian schools: Executive summary.
9. Jordan, M. (2022). Generation Expendable? Older women workers in the pandeconomy. www.grassrootsresearch.com.au.
10. Occupational Health & Safety.
11. This data was reported in 2014 but relates to 2009–2011 statistics.
12. We Are Union Reps. (Undated). Bullying - how much of a problem is it? https://www.ohsrep.org.au/bullying_-_how_much_of_a_problem_is_it.
13. OECD data cited in https://www.unisa.edu.au/unisanews/2019/september/story3/.
14. Powell, R. ABC News report. (2016). https://www.abc.net.au/news/2016-10-09/half-all-australians-experience-workplace-bullying-survey-finds/7916230?utm_campaign=abc_news_web&utm_content=link&utm_medium=content_shared&utm_source=abc_news_web. Accessed March 2022.

15. Magee, C., Gordon, R., Caputi, P., Oades, L., Reis, S., & Robinson, L. (2014). Workplace bullying in Australia. *Centre for Health Initiatives, University of Wollongong*.
16. Faa, M. (2019). Workplace bullying continues to affect thousands of Australians. ABC News, Nov 11, 2019. https://www.abc.net.au/news/2019-11-07/workplace-bullying-continues-to-affect-thousands-of-australians/11671062.
17. Safe Work Australia. (2021). Psychosocial health and safety and bullying in Australian workplaces. https://www.safeworkaustralia.gov.au/sites/default/files/2021-06/D21%209238%20Psychosocial_health_and_safety_and_bullying_in_australian_workplaces_6th_edition.pdf. p. 2.
18. Vveinhardt, J. & Streimikiene, D. (2016). Management culture and mobbing in a social organisation: whether a special status provides a guarantee of safety. Economic Research, 29:1, 950–966, https://doi.org/10.1080/1331677X.2016.1198981.
19. Schwindt, R. (2019). What Is Mobbing and How It Can Damage Our Mental Health and Well-being. https://www.psychreg.org/what-is-mobbing/. Accessed Aug 2021.
20. Kotz, D. (2003). Neoliberalism and the US Economic Expansion of the'90s. Monthly Review-New York-, 54(11), 15–33.
21. Antonio, R. J. (2013). Plundering the commons: The growth imperative in neoliberal times. The Sociological Review, 61, 18–42.
22. Crotty, J. (2000). Slow growth, destructive competition, and low road labor relations: A Keynes-Marx-Schumpeter analysis of neoliberal globalization.
23. Treadway, D.C., Shaughnessy, B.A., Breland, J.W., Yang, J., & Reeves, M. (2013). Political skill and the job performance of bullies. Journal of Managerial Psychology, 28(3), 273–289.
24. Antrobus, P. (2004). The Gift Economy inside and outside Patriarchal Capitalism conference. A Radically Different World View is Possible. https://youtu.be/4Fl0eimvRl4. Audio recording accessed Dec 2021.

CHAPTER 4

A Tale of Two Economies

Abstract With the pandemic bringing serious health risks for many workers, this chapter examines the role of 'Australia's sexist and bullying culture' in workplace practices that are not always gender neutral. Following the exposure of systemic workplace harassment in Australia's foremost workplace of federal Parliament House, a subsequent Australian Human Rights Commission inquiry had highlighted the role that rigid hierarchical structures can play in reproducing conditions of work that not only disadvantage women, but other groups more vulnerable to disadvantage and discrimination. The author links value propositions in Australia's labour market back to the time of invasion and colonisation, when European patriarchal capitalism superseded the more regenerative and circular 'gift economy' practices of Australia's First Nations peoples, as colonisation had succeeded in doing with pre-modern and Indigenous societies the world over.

Keywords Gift economy • Exchange capitalism • Systemic disadvantage • Discrimination • Workplace • Bullying • Gender • Pandemic • Exchange economy • Decolonise • Degrowth

M. Jordan, *Women's Work in the Pandemic Economy*,
https://doi.org/10.1007/978-3-031-40154-1_4

Introduction

Working the pandemic frontline had a significant impact upon women's health and wellbeing. In addition to the formal statistics relating to anxiety and depression noted in Chap. 1, *Generation Expendable?* revealed additional impacts upon women's wellbeing, impacts, survey responds told us, which came as a direct result of their experiences at work (see Fig. 4.1).

Gendered Bullying

That there was a gendered dimension to women's workplace experiences, including an apparent commonality of female-to-female aggression in feminised labour environments, reflects broader cultural settings relating to gender stereotypes and discrimination, which can be seen to pervade multiple areas of Australian life.

Just prior to Australia's first lockdown, the Australian Human Rights Commission (AHRC), had released *Respect@Work: Sexual Harassment National Inquiry Report* following complaints of harassment, bullying and *even sexual assault* in the country's uppermost workplace: Federal Parliament House.[1]

In the wake of a global '#MeToo' movement which was continuing to expose routine 'misconduct' from (mostly) men in (mostly) positions

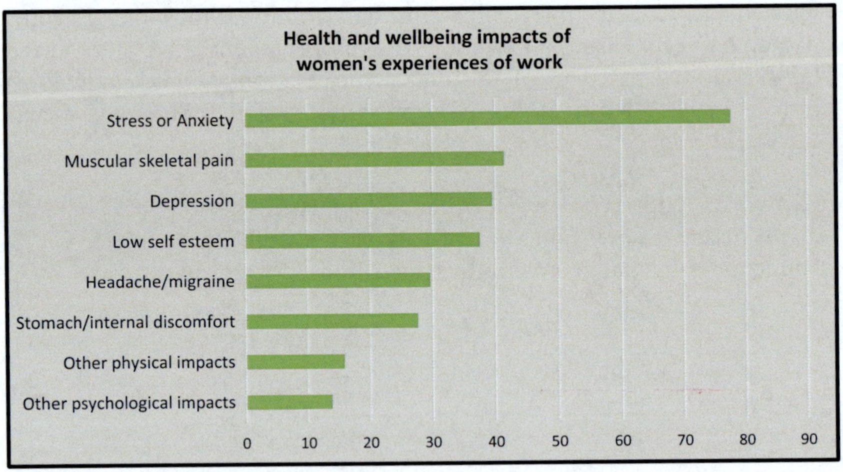

Fig. 4.1 Health impacts of the 'toxic workplace' on women workers

of power, the AHRC report highlighted just how far Australia 'lags behind other countries in preventing and responding to sexual harassment'. The report emphasised that harassment is much more probable in workplaces with rigid hierarchical structures.[2,3,4]

It also described the ways in which 'cultural and systemic drivers' shape work conditions: a configuration long-noted by agencies tackling Australia's skyrocketing rates of violence against women. *Respect@Work* stressed the urgent need for 'primary preventions' to tackle Australia's sexist and bullying culture:

> Actions must be taken by governments, organisations and individuals in the different settings where people live, work, learn and socialise … using a whole-of-community approach to address different aspects of the problem across multiple settings, including workplaces, media, education, arts, and sports.[5]

A Bullying Predisposition?

Generation Expendable? had exposed toxic work cultures as apparently common in the female-dominated occupations, including seemingly routine incidence of women bullying other women. While some might attribute this to a biologically inherent disposition of female 'bitchiness' or competitiveness: that nurses really do 'eat their young', this essentialist argument neglects broader cultural settings of a country still steeped in its colonial legacy.[6,7] Here, the health and education sectors, as with other institutions dating back to 'settlement', were topping bullying statistics well before COVID:[8,910,11,12]

> Systemic racism and discrimination [were] rooted in the structure of society itself, in governments, the workplace, courts, police and education institutions. Indeed, for women workers historically… the professional structure of higher education provided restricted employment, career, and leadership opportunities … exacerbated where there is an intersection between gender and race, culture, religion, or age.[13]

That there is a gender configuration to Australia's modern workplace structures is hard to deny, with workload burden a particular and well documented issue in the female-dominated health and education industries.[14,15,16] Aged care for example, a mostly privatised sector with both a feminised staff *and* a predominantly female client base, saw significantly higher rates of COVID contagion, death and staff shortages than any other sector. While the escalated disease burden in aged care was of course partly attributable to the vulnerable resident cohort, there were also notedly lax protections during the pandemic for both residents and workers. Even in 2023, aged care residents in Australia have 'alarming low' vaccination rates.[17,18,19]

As the literature reports:

> Organizations are not gender-neutral...Feminist institutionalism, a paradigm of 'new institutionalism', argues that in every organization, both formal and informal institutions in the form of rules, practices and narratives, are gendered.[20]

Traditionally, psychological ontologies have informed our understanding of, and therefore responses to, workplace bullying. Yet if we examine the findings of *Generation Expendable?* using a less individualised approach such as 'labor process theory', we can see that bullying is not only *tolerated* in female-dominated occupations, but effectively *structured in* through workload liability, systemic under-resourcing, hierarchical structures which favour males/male-coded behaviours and workforce fragmentation.

As neoliberal labour values increasingly expose all workers to highly pressured conditions, taking one's tension out on subordinates at work may present an almost *logical* recourse for women. When we further consider the broader context of Australia's still patriarchal culture, a nation wherein women still often experience some degree of inequality, disempowerment or even dominance in their domestic/private sphere, it is perhaps then unsurprising that any power imbalance women experience in the home may become an encumbrance they 'bring to work' and then transfer onto other women, particularly those who seem to challenge their authority, or capability in managing work responsibilities.

Under what now can only be described as the economic fundamentalism of late-stage capitalism therefore, women workers not only routinely experience conditions where it is 'okay to bully, harass and threaten', but also contribute to such conditions.[21] The coronavirus crisis has simply ameliorated and exposed already poor conditions of work in which bullying had become a 'rational form of behavior selectively employed by managers to influence behaviors and performance'; even a 'political tactic'.[22,23,24]

While some will still argue that the gendered bullying identified in Generation Expendable? study is biologically inherent to the female gender, under very different conditions, or economic environments of work, in a model which I will argue is aligned with 'degrowth futures', we see a very different presentation of women's labour in the pandemic economy.[25,26]

History of the Gift

Before presenting the findings of this second study of female labour taking place during the pandemic of 2020 and 2021, it is expedient to give an overview of what a 'gift economy' is, and its interrelationship to degrowth theory.

The first Western exploration of gifting cultures came in a 1923 essay by Marcel Mauss. Mauss employed anthropological and sociological epistemologies to depict Indigenous cultures in Polynesia, Melanesia and the American Northwest.[27] Mauss recorded activities across the economic, ceremonial and kinship structures of these pre-colonial societies, which he noted focused not only on the exchange of 'economically useful' goods, but also on '*ceremonies, feasts, rites, military services … dances, celebrations, fairs … very different systems of exchange from a European capitalist model*'.[28] Mauss described these pre-modern cultural practices as, '*phenomena of exchange and contract as characterised by gift-giving and reciprocity*'.[29]

In a modern interpretation, sociologist Terry Leahy explains:

> The gift economy is a reversal of key aspects of capitalism and class societies in general … Producing focuses on use for oneself or known others, whether locals, kin or friends … The structure pays off as a total system to benefit all of us. Gifts are necessary for everyone to live well. It is treasured as a system that works better than alternatives, which have already been tried with such calamitous effects.[30]

To an extent, these gifting customs remain common even under late-stage capitalism, expressed by gift economy advocate Genevieve Vaughan as humanity's 'homo donas', or gifting propensity, something that is routinely erased or rendered invisible in the (post)modern era, with its fundamental structures and accompanying discourse of capitalist cultures being one of 'exchange'; what Vaughan depicts as the 'exchange paradigm'.[31]

Gift Versus Exchange

While delineated gift economies may be hard to find in today's market globalism, decolonial feminists, Indigenous and degrowth scholars are illuminating the fundamental role that gifting still plays, underpinning exchange capitalism, in what some characterise as a 'feminine' or female-coded expression, one exemplified in women's 'gift' of unpaid caregiving and reproductive (house and childrearing at minimum) work. Yet a gifting also present in Mother Nature's unrecompensed resources, with the gifting of these feeding the pyramid of capital from the bottom up, and yet ignored in calculations of 'gross domestic product' (GDP, the measure of wealth/value intrinsic to growth discourse).

With the modern world almost wholly organised by this 'exchange logic' of capitalism, what are often described as more circular and sustainable knowledge traditions/systems, Indigenous practices and what some describe as more 'feminine' modes of social organisation are hidden and, at the same time, plundered.

While money is indubitably the 'exchange equivalent' underpinning capitalism, the differences between a 'gift economy' model and 'exchange economics' don't only related to money. As Mark Bonchek explains, while both function as *systems of exchange*, market and gift economies differ in core ways:

> 1) Context: In a market economy, the focus is always on transactions. In a gift economy, the focus is on relationships.
> 2) Currency: In a market economy, people use money. In a gift economy, people use social currencies. The purpose is not to execute a transaction but to express a relationship. A gift economy is therefore *relational*, not *transactional*;
> 3) Status: In a gift economy, status is earned. In a market economy, status can be bought.[32]

In the coming chapters, I will explore these differences in the context of a comparative analysis of the *Generation Expendable?* study of paid women workers in the pandemic economy, and the gifted labour of women in a second study entitled *The Gift Highway*.

Decolonising and Degrowth

Decolonisation is a process intrinsic to many degrowth models. Typically a word used in the context of 'post'-colonialism, 'decolonisation' references the urgency of 'dismantling white supremacy in thought'. It speaks to the redressing of enduring, and often intergenerational harms resulting from the colonial—and neocolonial—era. It is a term increasingly used by both feminist and degrowth scholars and one which informs this analysis in a number of ways.

The resituating of First Nations' ways of knowing, being and doing, one characteristic of decolonisation, is core to tackling the increasing urgency of climate change. In so-called Australia, as in other places where pre-modern or Indigenous cultures are being recognised and increasingly valued we see Aboriginal and Torres Strait Islander socioeconomic practices which, have at their core, an elemental respect for 'country' from which processes of land stewardship and custodianship ensure sustainable and collective provisioning in concert with cyclical nature.[33]

The concept of decolonisation also has a broader mantle, that of reforming the binaries of 'othering' which are inherent to capitalism and work to promote and uphold 'Western' knowledges above the more traditional social formations of the global South.[34,35]

Decolonising also has an important role to play in the context of the labour market and workplace. In Australia, it must first address the barriers to decent work and from there, equitable life opportunities, that Aboriginal and Torres Strait Islander people still typically face. Barriers which continue to drive a serious gap in longevity between Indigenous and non-Indigenous Australians.

Decolonisation also resonates in addressing systemic drivers of disadvantage: the institutional structures and workplace hierarchies that are based on mainstream Australian values and market definitions of 'success'. To decolonise growth capitalism necessarily involves the dismantling of the dichotomies of the system, at its most conspicuous perhaps, race and gender binaries.

If we are to address the toxicity of typical (Australian) workplace culture, we need to call out the power relations inherent to the system. Advocacy group Indigenous X tells us that the decolonising of any organisation 'must be intentional, resourced and based on ethical, moral and legal motivations for workplaces to learn and apply respectful ways of ensuring Indigenous self-determination and institution-wide responsibility.'

It is only in distinct and overt practices of decolonisation then, that we open up the possibility of (re)awakening the circular, reciprocal and gift economy practices that degrowth advocates believe offer us a path away from the destructive dynamisms of the growth paradigm.

Before introducing the findings of *The Gift Highway* study, it is useful to list the dualisms of the two opposing economies about which I write;

Gifting/Gift economy paradigm	Exchange Capitalism
Requires abundance and also creates it	Requires and creates scarcity (for leverage)
Implies an imbalance towards others	Requires balance in binary interactions – quid pro quo exchange
Relations of mutuality and trust	Debt and obligation, servitude, suspicion
Community interdependence	Separation, fragmentation, independence
The need calls forth the gift	One must 'deserve' to receive
Gives to market unwittingly	Takes from givers, denying and obscuring the real source
Truth telling	Lies and subterfuge
Integrity, self-confidence	Guilt, payback
Forgiving	Vengeance
Peace	War.

Fig. 4.2 Genevieve Vaughan's core binaries for differentiating gift and exchange economies

the characteristics which differentiate the 'growth' from the 'gift' paradigm (see Fig. 4.2).[36]

Decolonial feminist and degrowth scholar Mariam Abazeri writes about the *resistive* nature of degrowth practices in challenging colonial capitalism:

> In this resistance, practices, values, and norms that produce everyday habits, rhythms, economies, and senses of space and time are reappropriated away from a dichotomous and hierarchized fragmentation of the colonized self, creating space for multiple expressions and organizations of subjective and intersubjective relations. Intersectional analysis challenges understandings of power and domination at the nexus of race, class, gender and sexuality … decolonial feminisms moves away from dichotomous understandings of being that divide the human from non-human, the gendered from non-gendered, colonizers/'whites' from colonized/'people of color', away from powerful fictions towards a praxis of more plural and fluid understandings of being.[37]

In This Chapter …

The impacts of neoliberal values on workers were already starting to show prior to the onset of the coronavirus pandemic. They were characterised by increased workload and the sharpening of external and internal stressors for workers, with Australia's typical workplace settings inadequate in protecting, and/or meeting the needs of workers. Burnout, job dissatisfaction and bullying work cultures already common in Australia were only exasperated by the crisis and are sadly now driving the exodus of women workers from the feminised industries of care.

In the Next Chapter …

With pandemic lockdowns reshaping local communities, engagement in locally focused online networks offered women a different economy for caregiving.

Notes

1. Australian Human Rights Commission. (2020). Respect@Work: National Inquiry into Sexual Harassment in Australian Workplaces. https://humanrights.gov.au/sites/default/files/document/publication/ahrc_respectwork_community_guide_2020.pdf. Accessed Jan 2021.
2. Australian Human Rights Commission. (2020). Community Guide: Respect@Work: National Inquiry into Sexual Harassment in Australian Workplaces. p. 3. https://humanrights.gov.au/sites/default/files/document/publication/ahrc_respectwork_community_guide_2020.pdf. Accessed Jan 2021.
3. Australian Human Rights Commission. (2020). Respect@Work National Inquiry into Sexual Harassment in Australian Workplaces Report Summary. pp. 243 and 264.
4. Australian Human Rights Commission. (2020). Respect@Work: National Inquiry into Sexual Harassment in Australian Workplaces Report Summary. p. 443.
5. Ibid. (Citing submission references: Victorian Health Promotion Foundation (VicHealth), Submission 147, Sexual Harassment Inquiry, 11; Our Watch, Submission 281, Sexual Harassment Inquiry, 15–16; Victoria Legal Aid, Submission 283, Sexual Harassment Inquiry, 20; Women's Health Victoria, Submission 342, Sexual Harassment Inquiry, 4; Australian Chamber of Commerce and Industry, Submission 349, Sexual Harassment Inquiry, 10, 13.)
6. Kark, R. et al. (2023). Catty, bitchy, queen bee or sister? A review of competition among women in organizations from a paradoxical-coopetition perspective. 27 January 2023. https://doi.org/10.1002/job.2691.
7. American Association of Post-acute Care Nursing. (2021). Why Nurses Eat Their Young and How to Stop this Damaging Practice. AAPACN Online, Feb 23, 2021. Aapacn.org/article/why-nurses-eat-their-young-and-how-to-stop-this-damaging-practice/. Accessed March 2021.
8. These include the police and the military, as well as education and healthcare. NB, the Anti-bullying Reports of the Fair Work Commission are no longer published online. The archived link is here: https://web.archive.org/web/20220119182539/https://www.fwc.gov.au/about-us/reports-publications/quarterly-reports.

9. Schofield, T. (2009). Gendered organizational dynamics: the elephant in the room for Australian allied health workforce policy and planning? Journal of Sociology, 45(4), pp. 383–400.
10. Tuckey, M. Li, Y., Neall, A., Chen, P., Dollard, M., McLinton, S., Rogers, A., and Mattiske, J. (2022). Workplace bullying as an organizational problem: Spotlight on people management practices. Journal of Occupational Health Psychology, 27(6), 544–565. https://doi.org/10.1037/ocp0000335.
11. Collyer, F., Willis, F. and Lewis, S. (2017). Gatekeepers in the healthcare sector: Knowledge and Bourdieu's concept of field, Social Science & Medicine, Volume 186, 2017, Pages 96–103, ISSN 0277-9536, https://doi.org/10.1016/j.socscimed.2017.06.004.
12. Ferguson, H., & Anderson, J. (2021). Viewpoint: Professional dominance and the oppression of the nurse: The health system hierarchy. Australian Nursing and Midwifery Journal, Vol 27(Issue 4), 30–31. https://search.informit.org/doi/10.3316/informit.885233849666615.
13. New South Wales Government. (Last updated Mar 2023). History of New South Wales government schools. https://education.nsw.gov.au/about-us/our-people-and-structure/history-of-government-schools/government-schools/public-instruction-act-1880. Accessed Apr 2023.
14. Hegney, D., Plank, A. and Parker, V. (2003). Nursing workloads: the results of a study of Queensland nurses. Journal of nursing management, *11*(5), pp. 307–314.
15. MacDonald, T. (2020). Women are bearing the brunt of COVID pain in higher ed. Agenda, 28, pp. 16–17.
16. Willis, E., Toffoli, L., Henderson, J. and Walter, B. (2009). Gendered Relations to Working Time: Enterprise Bargaining Outcomes in Acute Care and Community Nursing Settings in Australia.
17. Dinh, H., Strazdins, L. and Welsh, J., (2017). Hour-glass ceilings: Work-hour thresholds, gendered health inequities. *Social Science & Medicine*, *176*, pp. 42–51.
18. Raciti, M., (2010). Marketing Australian higher education at the turn of the twenty-first Century: A précis of reforms, commercialisation and the new university hierarchy. E-Journal of Business Education & Scholarship of Teaching, 4(1).
19. McDonald, P., Thorpe, K. and Irvine, S., (2018). Low pay but still we stay: Retention in early childhood education and care. *Journal of Industrial Relations*, *60*(5), pp. 647–668.
20. Galea, N., Powell, A., Loosemore, M. and Chappell, L., (2020). The gendered dimensions of informal institutions in the Australian construction industry. Gender, work & organization, *27*(6), pp. 1214–1231.

21. Akella, D. (2016). Workplace bullying: Not a manager's right? SAGE Open, 6(1), 2158244016629394. p. 3.
22. Blackstock, S., Salami, B., & Cummings, G. G. (2018). Organisational antecedents, policy and horizontal violence among nurses: An integrative review. Journal of Nursing Management, 26(8), 972–991.
23. Akella, D. (2016). Workplace bullying: Not a manager's right? SAGE Open, 6(1), 2158244016629394. p. 3. (Citing Cortina, 2008 and Hutchinson & Jackson, 2014, p. 17).
24. Akella, D. (2016). Workplace bullying: Not a manager's right? SAGE Open, 6(1), 2158244016629394. (Citing Ferris, Zinko, Brouer, Buckley, & Harvey, (2007), as cited in Hutchinson et al., (2010), p. 29; and Cortina, (2008), p. 3.).
25. Nelson, A., & Edwards, F. (2020). Food for degrowth. In *Food for Degrowth* (pp. 1–16). Routledge.
26. Kish, K., & Quilley, S. (2017). Wicked dilemmas of scale and complexity in the politics of degrowth. *Ecological Economics*, *142*, 306–317.
27. Mauss, M. (1923). Cited in Stanford Education The Pioneer Sociologist Marcel Mauss on Gifts and Exchange Essay on the Gift: Forms and Motives of Exchange in Archaic Societies, 1923. https://web.stanford.edu/class/ihum54/odyssey/mauss_gift.htm.
28. Mauss, M. (Cited). Ibid.
29. Mauss, M. (Cited). Ibid.
30. Leahy, T. (2012). Cited in Gifting Economies. Arena, 2012. https://arena.org.au/gifting-economies/. Accessed August 2022.
31. Vaughan, G. (2023). Maternal Gift Salon #37. https://www.maternal-gifteconomymovement.org/salon-37-the-gift-of-communication/. Accessed March 2023.
32. Bonchek, M. (2012). How to Thrive in Social Media's gift Economy, *Harvard Business Review* https://hbr.org/2012/08/understanding-social-medias-gi. Accessed August 2022.
33. Moore, C. Caring for country: art as a platform for Indigenous and Western; land stewardship-Australian perspectives. *Sharing Cultures 2013*, 85.
34. Dudgeon, P. (2020). Decolonising psychology: Self-determination and social and emotional well-being 1. In *Routledge handbook of critical indigenous studies* (pp. 100–113). Routledge.
35. Phillips, G., and Hirvonen, T. (2021). Decolonisation of the workplace! Is more important than ever. Indigenous X, 17 Nov 2021. https://indigenousx.com.au/decolonisation-of-the-workplace-is-more-important-than-ever/. Accessed Nov 2021.

36. Vaughan, G. (2022). Salon #32 Marx, the Market and the Mother, May 7, 2022 (26 mins) https://www.maternalgifteconomymovement.org/salon-32-marx-the-market-and-the-mother/.
37. Abazeri, M. (2022). Decolonial Feminisms and Degrowth. Futures Volume 136, February 2022, 102902. pp. 2–3.

CHAPTER 5

Working by Gaslight

Abstract This chapter focuses on the 'social glue' of women's unpaid work, specifically, the 'gift economy behaviours' taking place on hyper-local digital sharing platforms during 2020 and 2021, as recorded in the author's second study of women workers in the pandemic economy. In stark contrast to workers in the paid economy, the women of *The Gift Highway* are engaged in provisioning both material and non-material items to their local community, in gift economy 'workspaces' which operate 'beyond money'. Here, women's labour is marked by authentic communication, collective responsibility and an ethos of conviviality that is very different to the 'toxic' relationships of care capitalism, where workers routinely reported experiences of being 'gaslighted', an institutionalised form of lying some Indigenous scholars link to patriarchal capitalism.

Keywords Gaslighting • The big lie • COVID • Gift economy • Volunteering • Carers • Sustainability • Hyper-local • Platform economy • Caregiving • Digital economy • Gifting • Money

Introduction

In the introduction to this book, I wrote that the research within told of two economies of women's labour taking place during the coronavirus pandemic. *Generation Expendable?* respondents had described the bullying

M. Jordan, *Women's Work in the Pandemic Economy*,
https://doi.org/10.1007/978-3-031-40154-1_5

work cultures of care capitalism. Would the second study, *The Gift Highway*, reveal a similar social environment at the frontline of unpaid care?

Would the competition, resentments and workload comparisons between women workers be equally discernible in what I was theorising was a gift economy model of caregiving labour? If so, then perhaps there was after all, something inherent to (female) gender, whether biologically or socially constituted, that rewarded female-to-female aggression over presentations of a universalised sisterhood.

Or might 'women's care work' recorded on hyper-local sharing platforms instead reveal gift economy labours characterised by support, caregiving, collective responsibility and convivial relationships?

The Social Glue

Prior to COVID, Australia was a nation with high volunteering rates: one in three Australians undertook voluntary work in 2019 with 2.5 million of those providing unpaid 'carer support' in the community. This unpaid 'workforce is also highly feminised, with seven out of ten unpaid carers female.[1,2]

The impact of COVID-19 on formal volunteering rates was instantaneous. Two thirds of Victorian voluntary programs had halted by April 2020; a loss equivalent to 12.2 million hours *per week*, with an estimated replacement value of $77.9 billion *per year*.[3,4]

With so many in-home and community-based supports cancelled, by August 2020, peak body Carers Australia had called for support, stating:

> This diligent provision of care, often in isolation, has been of benefit in combatting community transmission and should be acknowledged by government not just with words but with adequate financial support.[5]

Like women's 'gift' of unpaid work in the home, this typically gendered, voluntary work is not always valued. Much remains hidden, with formal statistics 'self-reported' and therefore likely to only comprise the tip of the iceberg, necessarily excluding the many millions of *micro-interactions* of support and connection: what I have previously described as *the social glue*.[6]

Leonora Risse explains:

> Activities that we previously outsourced to the market economy … we are probably now doing at higher volumes due to the pandemic. Behind the scenes … there are still millions of hours of unpaid and voluntary work taking place within our homes and communities … And it's no coincidence

> that the vast bulk of all forms of care – caring occupations in the paid workforce, unpaid domestic work undertaken at home, and volunteer service offered in communities – is done by women.[7]

As the pandemic impacted upon Naarm, and 'market' capitalism largely shut down, the need for human care and human connection only grew.

Virtual Caregiving

In recent years, hyper-local virtual communities have burgeoned in popularity. While some function as a sort of community notice board, many also have a focus on sustainable living, offering a platform for members to share, trade and recycle unwanted goods.[8] The sort of 'circular economic behaviours' associated with degrowth.

Internationally, '*BuyNothing*' and '*Transition*' (Towns) are platforms which attract millions to their local chapters typically sited on Facebook but in recent times, some moving away from the tech giant towards more ethical, app-based technology.[9]

In a similar vein to *local exchange trading systems* (LETS), *community exchange systems* (CETs) and the Swiss model 'timebanking', each of these 'new economies' focus on reciprocal exchange and sustainable living, encouraging behaviours which challenge the settings of growth capitalism.[10,11,12] In Australia, hyper-local sharing networks have also mushroomed, with homegrown examples such as *Hard Rubbish Rescue and Zero Waste Freebies* competing with more established groups.

Good Karma

Having investigated women's paid employment during COVID, I wanted to also explore women's *unpaid* care work during COVID. I decided to focus on Naarm-based not-for-profit group *The Good Karma Effect* (GKE). I chose this hyper-local community because, rather than simply functioning as a sustainable trading platform, it additionally mandates a focus on positive and caring interactions, as the GKE mission attests:

> Passing on good karma through 'location-based, safe, online communities for neighbours to connect, share resources and find positive solutions to each other's challenges', with a mission to provide the framework and support to enable passionate community members to facilitate positive outcomes.[13]

Methodology: The Gift Highway

Utilising a similar methodology to that used for *Generation Expendable? The Gift Highway* study involved the gathering of both quantitative and qualitative data relating to member interactions in three Good Karma Networks (GKNs) based in metropolitan Naarm, from a total of 35+ networks across Australia.[14]

Operating beyond money' and therefore what I hypothesised might be outside of market capitalism's 'exchange logic', I recorded all COVID-keyword-responsive posts occurring across 2020 and 2021, to analyse within a set of research criteria which I hoped would determine whether the extent to which activities on the GKNs might align with degrowth/post-capitalist models, specifically with what is described as the gift economy paradigm.[15]

Accordingly, posts were organised into the following 'gifting' categories:

- A request for information or advice: a '*non-material gift request*';
- A request for goods or services: *a* '*material gift request*';
- A post offering free items, '*gifting material goods or services*';
- A post offering a '*non-material gift*', loosely, i.e., a gift of communication or information relevant to the pandemic.

As with the first study, I applied a theoretic lens of degrowth, and of linked (decolonial) feminisms to inform my analysis as to whether the networks might constitute a second and unpaid care 'workplace' of feminised labour, and if so, whether the three online groups might then be considered micro gifting economies which aligned with core degrowth tenets.

Posts were also categorised according to the (apparent) gender of the poster, and whether the post was specific to the coronavirus and/or lockdown measures. The number of 'reactions' (Facebook emojis), and the number of responses that each post received were also noted.

Without any way in which to apportion the motive of persons posting—or commenting—on the forum, the intention was once again to simply 'snapshot' the 'labours' taking place and from there, to contrast this unpaid community workplace with the 'toxic' care cultures of neoliberalism.[16]

In total, 764 posts across the three GKNs were recorded and analysed, and a small number of case studies/interviews undertaken. In addition, The Good Karma Effect board generously granted access to two member surveys, dated August 2020 and October 2022.

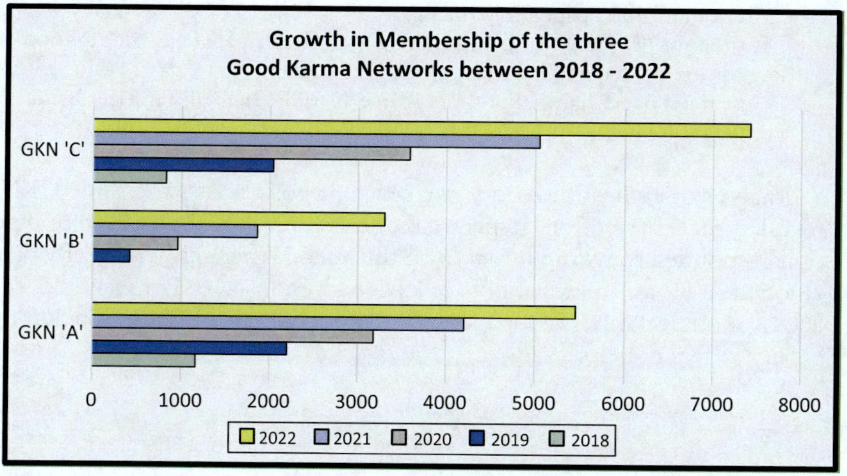

Fig. 5.1 Membership growth in the three selected GKNs, 2018–2022

Care in the Time of Corona

The Good Karma Networks had attracted membership into the thousands prior to COVID, but under lockdown conditions which saw tens of thousands of residents newly tied to their local community, GKE membership grew quite substantially (see Fig. 5.1).[17]

Material Gifting

As in countries across the world, the shock of the pandemic and imminent government restrictions triggered a run on 'essential' household items in Australia. The inability to effortlessly source goods was as horrifying to Australians as to most people of the global North. The attendant panic was notable across all three GKNs, from the initial March 2020 lockdown right through to 2021, when Rapid Antigen Tests (RATs) had replaced facemasks and toilet paper as unexpectedly 'desirable' items:

> I run a dance school and we are almost out of toilet paper. We have 100+ kids each week and each cubicle is down to its last roll. The church will also be here on Sunday with an elderly congregation. If anyone has any spare (please only if it isn't an inconvenience!) it would be greatly appreciated.[18]

> In need of toilet paper help plz.
> I thought people were joking there was no toilet paper! it's not a good time for me as i have to have surgery in the morning
> Any toilet paper hacks? Food isnt scarce anymore but still can't get hands on this. Please help.

Analysis of each of the pandemic keyword posts across the three GKNs revealed that these often desperate requests for material goods were typically responded to within hours, with the material item either directly provisioned or a 'non-material gift' of advice given instead. For example, the above quote seeking 'toilet paper hacks' attracted 66 comments, including explicit offers of help.

Non-material Gifting

In addition to responding to the material needs of others, GKN members also posted unsolicited offers of support:

> Is anyone running low on toilet paper? I can spare a few rolls. What is wrong with people and this ridiculous stockpiling?!
> Anyone desperate for toilet paper? I'm particularly thinking of people who can't get to the shops. I have a few spares. 👍

The swiftness and severity of the lockdown restrictions prompted a number of GKN members to think about others in their community, particularly people who might be isolated and vulnerable:

> I'm worried about older people, those who can't access shops and with hardly any family to help out or not a lot of money. How can we support people?

Analysis of all 764 keyword-responsive posts revealed a model that, like other neighbourhood/sharing platforms, offered members a place to share goods. The GKNs however, were also a place where pandemic-specific information and support could be offered and shared—support that couldn't always be easily sourced in the real world. With strict limitations on the duration and distance from home that residents of metropolitan Naarm were allowed, this need for up-to-date and local information was often pressing.

In the first months of 2020, questions and updates relating to local case numbers, local exposure sites, and local testing sites were common:

> Looking for a COVID testing centre with a fast turnaround time – hopefully same day …? 🦠😩 Thank you
>
> Anyone got a hot tip on the best place to get a quick result COVID test?
>
> Is anyone aware of COVID breakouts in local schools? XXXX College has been unlucky and is closed for deep cleaning and tracing.
>
> Does anyone know where the known cases of Covid-19 in XXXX originated?
>
> A covid-positive person travelled on the XXX train last Thursday morning … in case you were on that tram.

With the GKE model responding to both urgent and sometimes *collective* need for goods and information, and with COVID-related posts dominating the platforms well into 2021, it was apparent that the networks functioned as the sort of (real life) community notice board once provided by local governments in Australia. While outside the scope of this study, a quick comparison between COVID-related posts in one of the GKNs analysed, and the corresponding geographical area's city council Facebook page, showed the latter attracting far less engagement around the pandemic (restrictions), despite boasting twice the number of followers.[19,20]

With lack of trust in government an issue for Australia even before 2020, it seemed that COVID updates shared by local people, outside of any apparent political context, better responded to members' preferences for trusted sources of 'hyper-local' and 'real-time' information than that of the government; i.e., news coming from the 'bottom-up'.[21]

Seeking 'Non-material Gifts'

With the Good Karma Effect mission emphasising 'positive interactions', the three GKNs also functioned as a virtual workplace of care provisioning. As Naarm's lockdowns endured, members seemed more confident—or more desperate—to express their needs and vulnerabilities.

The numerous requests for 'non-material gifts' that the study recorded often included a personal element:

> Stressed and anxious with lockdown! Asking for help to put my mind at ease … what can I do to remain as safe as possible?
>
> Have you been impacted by COVID? Maybe feeling isolated and lonely, or worried about what happens when the restrictions have been lifted?? This new group for people struggling to stay hopeful and connected might be for you! We understand this is a really difficult time and want you to know that

> you're all welcome! Group is run with counsellors and focuses on restoring hope – we would love to have you!
>
> Help! I have dislocated my shoulder and can't lift my arm – can anyone help?

Interestingly, member posts asking for support proved some of the most popular, attracting the highest rates of reaction and response. Sometimes an appeal for support was met by a single individual, however, network members were also often seen coming together in a sort of 'care collective' of 'hive mind' problem solving. These communal responses could range from a collective provisioning of goods, to multiple and often reciprocated 'non-material gifts' of encouragement and reassurance, such as sympathetic comments or simply 'virtual hugs'.

That local people committed time and energy to supporting other community members, *strangers*, voluntarily, and without the quid pro quo expectations of the monetary economy, seemed to create a very different, even diametrically opposed, workplace culture.

Instead of the stressed and often resentful individualisms seen in the businesses of care, GKN workers seemed instead to be 'other-focused' and generous in gifting their time, their thoughts and ideas, that is, in caregiving. So much so that, in a country whose national culture is deeply scored by neoliberalism, one proudly competitive and individualistic, the economic behaviours of the GKE gift economy model seemed almost *subversive in nature*.[22,23,24]

The Gift of Care

While a pressing need for income indisputably kept many Australian women in unsafe and unsatisfying jobs, it is important to note that a strong sense of vocation is also typical of people attracted to the teaching and caring professions.[25,26] With an increasingly corporatised model of 21st century care however, nurturing and compassionate workers may find themselves quite at odds with workplace settings focused mostly on 'efficiency' in a more fragmented than a holistic version of care-giving.

The 'person-centred', 'consumer-directed' care model typical of both Australia's public healthcare institutions and of private industry, allows little time for client/carer relationships to develop. Respectful and dignified interactions are often effectively structured out by an impossibly high burden of work, and by the itemisation of care into tasks which, in just one example, sees only 6 minutes allocated for a worker to shower a frail resident of aged care.[27]

That the GKNs operated as a workplace of caregiving during COVID can be seen in the high rates of engagement with care-seeking posts. It was also evident in the responses from the two GKE member surveys, relating, for example, to one question asking which activities on the platform members 'found most beneficial'.

In 2020, at the height of the pandemic, these were reported as:

1. Recycling/giving or receiving free items (68%);
2. Sharing information, education and advice (48%);
3. Problem resolution (asking for and receiving help) (37%);
4. Sharing humour, gratitude and other positive experiences (32%);
5. To find opportunities to help people and contribute (24%).

In the same survey, members' motivations for visiting/reading their local GKN newsfeed were similar:

1. Offering free items (69%);
2. Accepting free items (53%);
3. Providing recommendations for a local business/service (52%);
4. To experience/view positive interactions in the community (37.2%);
5. To find community events, activities, or information (33.9%);
6. To share free items/resources (30.1%);
7. To find opportunities to help people/contribute (24%).

In 2022, when communities had presumably adapted to 'COVID normal', it was interesting to note very little change in member motivation—bar one: a significant increase in appreciation for of free items, that is, *practices of gift-giving*:[28,29]

1. Offering free items (81%);
2. Sharing free items and resources (37%);
3. Ask(ing) for recommendations or assistance (37%);
4. To experience/view positive interactions in the community (32%);
5. To find community events, activities or information (31%);
6. Seeking free items/resources (26%);
7. To find opportunities to help people/contribute (24%).[30]

Additionally in 2022, one quarter of GKN members stated that they visited their network specifically '*to find opportunities to help people or contribute*':

> This group is a great place to reach out & connect with others in the area. This could be to ask for help when you're in a pickle, or needing some different perspectives on a problem, or looking for local recommendations or advice. It could be to find people with similar interests, to start a support group, or to find someone for a chat or a listening ear. If you are isolated, due to lockdown or for any reason, there are people here that can & want to help. We cannot know what other people need until they ask ... Thank you! VIRTUAL GROUP HUG

Both the keyword-post analysis and the member survey data strongly indicated that the GKNs offered members an alternative economy, one in which they could participate in gifting practices outside of exchange capitalism; an economy responding to people's needs in thoughtful and relational ways typically discouraged by the industries of care.

> I feel like the GKN does for my suburb what a local newspaper and a pub and a sporting club might have done in the past ... somewhere you can find nearly everyone, so it's possible to ask for or offer help, share information about local events, and mobilise the community when necessary. It's a particularly important resource for those who are a bit isolated or have not developed organic connections with their neighbours - we might not feel able to pop next door for a cup of sugar but asking for one on the GKN is somehow easier!

Beyond Money

The commoning infrastructure of the GKE model, its hyper-local and care-full focus, offered both the technical and the social settings which allowed members to support and connect with each other during COVID. Notably, the material gifting and gift requests that took place functioned wholly outside of capital production, instead recycling unwanted and used goods within the local area according to need. This often also included the lending of items: I myself borrowed an oil radiator for two weeks when our heating went down.

It seemed clear that, at least during COVID, lockdowns, residents converged in these virtual communities to find social connection and a space in which they could express personal concerns, tell stories and respond to the needs of others in a deeply local context; a community seemingly so '*beyond money*' as to imply that a '*decolonising of the growth imaginary*' might be taking place.[31,32]

Degrowth scholar Anitra Nelson argues that moving 'beyond money' is essential if humanity is to avert the worsening climate and related capitalist crises:

> Unless postcapitalism is money-free, we will fail to establish a world beyond capitalism. If money is the strategic organising principle of capitalism, then no money, no capitalists. Money is not only the form but also the seed of capital. Nonmonetary production and exchange – collective planning, commoning and sharing – undercut capitalists' power absolutely.[33]

For Nelson, money has an essential function in driving the hoarding of capital. She proposes that without money, we will have 'no capitalists', leaving humanity time to instead focus on:

> 'real values', as opposed to standardised and unitary monetary values which are encountered in the everyday world simply as prices.[34]

We see a similar focus from Indigenous scholar Mililani Trask. For Trask, an advocate for a gift economy model, the systemic change we so urgently need can only come through a recalibration of social values:

> The values underlying the globalised approach are consumption and individualism.... When you hear those terms, 'sustainability', 'preservation', you understand that it speaks to our collective social obligation and responsibility. {But] there is no understanding [of] the broader social obligation or responsibility that arises over the capitalist globalised economic system because the underlying values are individual and consumptive in nature.[35]

Indigenous and gift economy models differ from exchange capitalism in distinct ways, most particularly perhaps, in the absence of *competition* and presence of convivial relations of reciprocity.

For Trask:

> Reciprocity is a fundamental value of the gift economy. It is also a fundamental cornerstone of Indigenous communities. Reciprocity implies that there is an ebb and flow in relationships, a give and take. Reciprocity infers that there is a mutual sharing, something given for something taken. In Indigenous societies, reciprocity is the way things ... Reciprocity is not defined or limited by the language of the market economy because it implies that more is owed than financial payment when goods and services exchange hands.[36]

Working by Gaslight

Native American academic Barbara Alice Mann identifies *lying* as a principal weapon of colonisation, stating: '*Europeans ... have a very fraught relationship with telling the truth'*. In stark contrast, pre-colonial and Indigenous cultures were typically mutual; horizontal in their provisioning and decision-making protocols. For some degrowth and gift economy advocates, these Indigenous and pre-modern societies are interpreted as having 'matriarchal' formations, even though men and women might still have differentiated roles. This concept of truth-telling therefore, is characterised by some academics as being 'feminine'.[37]

Mann explains that, in American cultures prior to the arrival of Europeans lying was:

> Unthinkable, so unthinkable we literally did not think about it. This is why we wound up with about 400 treaties with the US government in which [they] kept...not one. Every single treaty was broken, so this is how we found out that Euro Christianity was paying lip service to the idea of telling the truth.[38]

For Mann, European colonisers and settlers employed lying as a strategy to destroy trust and exclude. She does not believe that lying is *accidental* to (coloniser) societies, rather, she sees it as a strategy 'culturally tied to patriarchy', with exclusionary societies 'primarily patriarchal' in nature. By contrast, pre-modern 'welcoming cultures', Mann describes as typically 'matriarchal'.

> Lying destroys trust, making it easier to frighten, and thus to control, people ... The reward for being part of the recognized in-crowd is the ability to participate in oppressing others .... And once you destroy people's trust you scare the heck out of them. Once they are frightened they are very easy to control.[39]

That the women workers at the pandemic frontline made a number of references to being 'gaslighted', a term describing processes of lying, manipulation and control originally coined in relation to intimate partner violence, but recently recognised for its institutional application, is perhaps telling.

In relation to employment, 'institutional gaslighting' is said to occur when harms such as bullying, harassment and assault are perpetrated within an institutional setting, and responded to by the workplace or employer silencing, or questioning 'the truth' of the victim/survivor, to ensure the protection of the place of work, or institution itself.[40,41,42]

In *Generation Expendable?*, we saw references to being 'gaslighted' in the case studies of both Rachel and Margot, and more broadly. In citing their experiences of 'inappropriate' and bullying behaviours, women often described work cultures which appeared to support, encourage, even *routinely practice* lying:

- The shifting of goalposts without telling you (52.4%);
- Freezing out, ignoring or excluding (47.6%);
- Constant undermining of your efforts (43.9%);
- Withholding necessary information from you (39%);
- Being the subject of malicious or unfair rumours (11.8%).

This *engendering* of lying in workplace cultures may be patriarchal in nature, but is not of course, solely specific to the *male gender*, as the accounts from *Generation Expendable?* attest. Sadly, that study indicated that 'gaslighting' and lying were often used as strategies for controlling workers, both in the pandemic workplace and also prior to COVID, with the truth routinely weaponised to keep workers in line. As Mann explains, an important outcome of this patriarchal/European practice culture is that 'lies makes the majority complicit in behavior that most would eschew as individuals.'[43]

In the 'micro economies' of Good Karma however, a quite different culture was apparent; one consistently open and inclusive, with the networks clearly offering members a safe space in which to express their needs, vulnerabilities and even, as we shall see, their 'authentic' selves.

In This Chapter ...

In this chapter, we have looked at the 'workspaces' of the GKNs during the pandemic, loosely comparing them with the industries of care capitalism, where the focus on pecuniary efficiencies means that even a convivial conversation between client and patient must be quantified and 'accounted' for. In sharp contrast, Naarm's GKNs offered members a trusted source of locally-focused and timely information; a platform where isolated residents could seek advice and support.

In the Next Chapter …

We look further into the cultures of the three GKNs during COVID, considering the extent to which they might be considered workplaces of care. If so, to what extent might the activities of caregiving and care receiving comprise a gift economy model and if so, whether this might constitute a gendered or *maternal* gift economy?

Notes

1. Australian Bureau of Statistics (2019). General Social Survey (GSS). https://www.aihw.gov.au/reports/australias-welfare/volunteers. Accessed Nov 2022.
2. Australian Bureau of Statistics. (2021). Unpaid work and care: Census data 2021. https://www.abs.gov.au/statistics/people/people-and-communities/unpaid-work-and-care-census/latest-release. Accessed Nov 2020.
3. Carers Australia. (2020). Replacement Value of Unpaid Care in Australia Rises To $77.9 Billion Per Year. 31 July 2020. https://www.carersaustralia.com.au/replacement-value-of-unpaid-care-in-australia-rises-to-77-9-billion-per-year/#:~:text=Replacement%20value%20of%20unpaid%20care%20in%20Australia%20rises%20to%20%2477.9%20billion%20per%20year,-31%20July%202,020&text=A%20new%20report%20commissioned%20by,was%20last%20conducted%20in%202,015. Accessed Nov 2020.
4. Centre for Social Research and Methods at the Australian National University. (ANU). (2021) Volunteering during the COVID-19 pandemic (April 2021). p. 4.
5. Deloitte Access Economics and Carers Australia. (2020). The value of informal care in 2020. May 2020. https://www.carersaustralia.com.au/wp-content/uploads/2020/07/FINAL-Value-of-Informal-Care-22-May-2020_No-CIC.pdf. Accessed Aug 2021.
6. Jordan, M. (2017) Money for Jam? Women's Agenda, September 2017. https://womensagenda.com.au/latest/28303/.
7. Risse, L. (2020). Undervalued and unseen: Australia's COVID-19 frontline workforce. Power 2 Persuade, April 14, 2020. https://www.powertopersuade.org.au/blog/undervalued-and-unseen-australias-covid-19-frontline-workforce/14/4/2020. Accessed June 2020.
8. Cited in Lake, M. (2009). Timeline: The evolution of online communities. https://www.computerworld.com/article/2526581/timeline%2D%2Dthe-evolution-of-online-communities.html. Accessed Jan 2020. Also cited in Davies, F. (Undated). https://www.techwalla.com/articles/the-history-of-chat-rooms Accessed Jan 2023.

9. Sato, M. (2022). Buy Nothing exploded on Facebook — now it wants a platform of its own. The Verge. https://www.theverge.com/tech/2022/1/12/22878353/buy-nothing-groups-facebook-app Accessed March 2023.
10. A more detailed definition of both LETS and CES can be seen at https://www.communityexchange.net.au/home/about/what-is-the-community-exchange-system/; and https://en.wikipedia.org/wiki/Local_exchange_trading_system.
11. Naughton-Doe, R., Cameron, A., and Carpenter, J. (2020). Timebanking and the co-production of preventive social care with adults; what can we learn from the challenges of implementing person-to-person timebanks in England? Health & Social Care in the Community, 29(5), pp. 1285–1295. https://doi.org/10.1111/hsc.13166.
12. Dreier, D. (2023). Time Banking and Time-Based Currency in Switzerland. Moneyland, May 10, 2023.https://www.moneyland.ch/en/time-banking-currency-switzerland-guide. Accessed May 2023.
13. The Good Karma Effect. https://www.goodkarmaeffect.com/about/good-karma-effect. Accessed August 2022.
14. The number changed as some closed and new networks opened across the research period.
15. Using Facebook's (limited) search engine, I recorded all unique posts responding to the pandemic-related keywords of 'covid', 'lockdown', 'toilet paper', 'RAT' and 'vaccine'. There were limitations and assumptions in this methodology. For example, the 'keyword' did not have to have been mentioned in the initial member post, to respond to the search, just mentioned in a response. This meant not all data recorded was relevant to the pandemic. It also meant some posts responded to more than one keyword and therefore duplicate entries were common, although removed where noted. The Facebook emoji 'reactions'—*like, love, dislike, laughter, crying and care*—were not broken down.
16. Classification of gender was based upon members' names. If not clear from there, publicly available photos where examined. In a very few cases only was the gender categorised as 'unclear'.
17. Defined as between March 2020 and 31st December 2022 for the purposes of this publication.
18. Quotes have been reworded to de-identify specific authors.
19. The geographically associated City Council's Facebook page had 11 K followers in December 2022. A similar keyword search found the following: 'Covid' + '2020' = 0 posts; 'Covid' + '2021' = 6 posts; 'Lockdown' + '2020' = 11 posts and 'Lockdown' + '2021' = 4/5 posts.
20. With the Victorian State Government holding daily media briefings during the first virus outbreak in Naarm, this may explain why local councils did little more than share official releases.

21. There is evidence that trust in Australian governments initially grew during 2020. See: https://qld.ipaa.org.au/2020/09/political-trust-and-democracy-in-times-of-coronavirus-is-australia-still-the-lucky-country/. Accessed March 2023.
22. Saluja, G. (2020). We're not all in this together. Messages about social distancing need the right cultural fit. The Conversation. April 8, 2020. https://theconversation.com/were-not-all-in-this-together-messages-about-social-distancing-need-the-right-cultural-fit-135427 https://theconversation.com/were-not-all-in-this-together-messages-about-social-distancing-need-the-right-cultural-fit-135427. Accessed March 2021.
23. Leaney, D. (2016). What is Australia's (business) culture? Strategium. LinkedIn, Feb 16, 2016. https://www.linkedin.com/pulse/what-australias-business-culture-david-leaney/. Accessed May 2021.
24. Vaughan, G. (2004). Heterosexism and the Norm of Normativity in Women and the Gift Economy: A Radically Different Worldview is Possible (edited by Genevieve Vaughan). p. 209.
25. Kersten, J., Bakewell, K., & Meyer, D. (1991). Motivating factors in a student's choice of nursing as a career. The Journal of nursing education, 30(1), 30–33. https://doi.org/10.3928/0148-4834-19910101-08.
26. Bergmark, U.; Lundström, F.; Manderstedt, L. and Palo, A. (2017). Why become a teacher? Student teachers' perceptions of the teaching profession and motives for career choice. European Journal of Teacher Education, pp. 266-281. Mar 07, 2018. https://doi.org/10.1080/02619768.2018.1448784. Accessed March 2023.
27. Ibrahim, J. (2018). What is 'quality' in aged care? The Conversation, Oct 24, 2018. https://theconversation.com/what-is-quality-in-aged-care-heres-what-studies-and-our-readers-say-104852. Accessed Nov 2020.
28. 'COVID normal' was marked by the opening up of the economy, QR code processes and the commencement of vaccination programmes.
29. There were only 1270 responses to the 2022 survey, compared with 3402 responses in 2020.
30. The Good Karma Effect. (2023). Unpublished data from the Good Karma Effect Member Surveys 2020 and 2022.
31. Hollo, T. (2022). Living Democracy: An ecological manifesto for the end of the world as we know it. UNSW Press. Accessed Nov 2022.
32. Leahy, T. (2022). System Change Made Simple. Buzzsprout. https://www.buzzsprout.com/2014361. Accessed Nov 2022.
33. Nelson. A. (2022). Beyond Money. Apple Books. p. 155.
34. Nelson, A. (2022). Ibid. p. 223.
35. Trask, M. (2020). Indigenous Women and Traditional Knowledge. Reciprocity is the Way of Balance in Women and the Gift Economy: A

Radically Different Worldview is Possible (edited by Genevieve Vaughan). p. 293.
36. Trask, M. (2020). Ibid.
37. Mann, B. A. (2007). In Vaughan, G. (Ed.). Women and the Gift Economy. A Radically Different Worldview is Possible. Inanna Publications and Education Inc. http://gift-economy.com/wordpress/wp-content/uploads/2013/08/womenandthegifteconomy.pdf. p. 3.
38. Mann, B. A. (2007). In Vaughan, G. (Ed.). Women and the Gift Economy. A Radically Different Worldview is Possible. Inanna Publications and Education Inc. http://gift-economy.com/wordpress/wp-content/uploads/2013/08/womenandthegifteconomy.pdf. p. 3.
39. Mann, B.A. (2011). Ibid.
40. Glambek, M. et al. (2014). Workplace bullying as an antecedent to job insecurity and intention to leave: A 6-month prospective study. Human Resource Management Journal, VL 24, (3), March 2014. DOI: 10.1111/1748-8583.12035.
41. Kennedy-Cuomo, M. (2019). Institutional Gaslighting: Investigations to Silence the Victim and Protect the Perp. Brown Review, April 5, 2019. https://brownpoliticalreview.org/2019/04/institutional-gaslighting-investigations-vane-silence-victim-protect-perp/.
42. Tuckey, M.R., Li, Y., Neall, A.M., Chen, P.Y., Dollard, M.F., McLinton, S.S., Rogers, A. and Mattiske, J., (2022). Workplace bullying as an organizational problem: Spotlight on people management practices. Journal of occupational health psychology, 27(6), p. 544.
43. Mann. Ibid. (2011).

CHAPTER 6

A Hidden Gift Economy?

Abstract While the workplaces of *Generation Expendable?* encouraged worker competition, individualism and an overburden of workload, (women's) behaviour taking place in the communities of the Good Karma Effect, a hyper-local digital sharing platform, suggests that the 'real values' referred to in degrowth and related anticapitalist theories still define Australian society—however, we just no longer organise our society in ways which support and promote these values. However, the interactions and activities taking place in the GKE model instead show that, when left (mostly) alone to organise, women typically come together in convivial communications, identifying common goals and expressing 'economic behaviours' that defy the so-called 'rational' selfishness of the exchange economy and instead encourage expressions of concern for others and an open generosity in sharing not only material goods, but also non-material gifts of personal experience, empathy and advice.

Keywords Gift-giving • Gift economy • Inclusion • Frugal abundance • Conviviality • Care-full • Open localisation • Localism • Degrowth • Place-based

M. Jordan, *Women's Work in the Pandemic Economy*,
https://doi.org/10.1007/978-3-031-40154-1_6

Introduction

The patterns which had emerged from *Generation Expendable?* suggest that there will likely be potential long-term financial impacts of the 'she-cession' for women in the older age cohorts in particular, as well as potential for *health consequences* as a result of their pandemic conditions of work.

The still-gendered landscape of caregiving, whether paid or unpaid labour, impacts nearly all women across their lifecourse, increasing women's vulnerability to disadvantage in a multitude of ways. Less frequently noted, this gendering of caregiving and of nurturing behaviours also disadvantages men.

Despite the pandemic bringing a rise in domestic work burdens for all, a 2021 survey of Australian men and women showed that while men's childcare time increased in relative terms during the early months of the crisis, the gap in housework between male and female family members remained steady, with women still carrying the much greater burden:

> While the lockdown generated lower subjective time pressure, dissatisfaction with balance of paid and unpaid work rose markedly and from a much higher base for women.[1]

The findings from *Generation Expendable?* which suggest that women workers routinely face quite significant occupational health and safety risks, and that 'market' settings in the caring sectors can also have a negative effect upon 'care recipients', suggest there is something fundamentally wrong in commodifying care.

In stark contrast, the activities of women taking place in what appeared to be a 'gift economy' model of the Good Karma Effect suggested that when left to self-organise, women typically interacted through convivial communications, identifying shared goals and displaying economic behaviours that defy the supposedly 'rational' and ego-focused selfishness of the exchange economy; its behavioural heuristics set at maximising personal outcomes and profit. Instead, *The Gift Highway* study recorded members showing concern for others, an open generosity in sharing not only material, but non-material goods of personal experience, empathy and advice. This caregifting that we see from the almost wholly female membership of the Good Karma Networks is fundamental to humanity, as degrowth discourse tells us.

Genevieve Vaughan writes:

> Consistent with traditions, the notion that many, many of us have been working on for decades, [is] that women's work must be respected and honoured and valued… But it mustn't be commodified. And there's a problem. Unless and until one can begin looking at a paradigm of giving and moving everything in that direction … not trying to keep a few areas that aren't commodified, but absolutely getting rid of the notion of exchange and a world built on that.[2]

My hypotheses in studying the interactions taking place on the three GKNs during the pandemic was firstly to consider whether they might comprise a gift economy. This would be proved by all, or a very high majority, of the keyword posts made during COVID fitting into one of the gift economy indicators developed, that are described in the previous chapter.

The second conjecture of the study was to assess the extent to which the GKNs might align with the core tenets of degrowth theory.

Thirdly, *The Gift Highway* study would examine the role of gender in these unpaid 'workplaces', seeking to identify any patterns of female-dominated and/or female-coded activities, consistent with what some degrowth feminists describe as 'care-full' practices or cultures.

A Gift Economy?

To assess whether the economic behaviours seen on the Good Karma Networks might be considered gift economy practices, each of the 764 keyword-responsive posts was analysed to see if its perceived underlying purpose might aligned with one or more of the chosen categories (see Fig. 6.1).

With the use of money, and even 'currencies' of swapping and trading explicitly 'designed out' under the GKE model, it was exciting to see members interacting and responding to both material and non-material needs without expectation of equivalence.

As the dominant category, it is pertinent to explain the rationale of the classification 'requests for non-material gifts' and how these requests for information, advice and support on the GKNs differed from pandemic information shared by both official agencies, and also what has been described as the 'infodemic' on social media during COVID.[3]

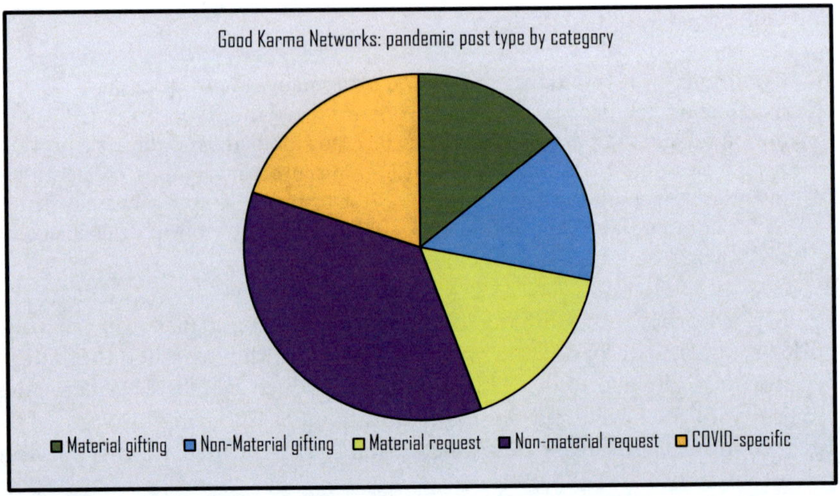

Fig. 6.1 Three GKNs: total pandemic keyword posts by 'gift economy' category

To understand the important role of communication to the gift economy model, it is useful to refer to the 'maternal' gift paradigm. Here, Genevieve Vaughan and other scholars describe language and communication as a defining element of gift-giving societies; sharply demarcating gifting practices from those of the market or exchange economy.

For Vaughan:

> Almost everything that you read about communication does call it an exchange. Instead, communication is really based on giving and receiving and we learn it in our earliest days from our mothers at the material level.[4]

Vaughan believes that, as a society, we need to begin to understand communication as giving and receiving of social relations, and not simply an exchange of information. She gives the example of communication between children and their motherers, which is often playful, a 'game of giving and receiving … not quid pro quo':

> And so you have this whole top down exchange way, where the one that has the most is the most important, and then you have a gift way where there is sharing and a kind of communication with each other that unites people instead of separating them, and it allows cooperation instead of competition.[5]

Vaughan describes modern capitalist society as a separating, rather than a commoning of human experience. This is because the main way that we communicate on our modern world is through exchange and transactionalism, economic behaviour '*which contradicts the very idea of gifting… we separate ourselves through exchange while we unite through giving and receiving.*'[6]

We see a similar augmenting of this 'immaterial work' from Susan Petrilli, a professor of philosophy and theory of languages. Petrilli describes communication and language not only as inseparable from gift giving, but '*in effect, is itself gift giving*'.[7]

Petrilli explains:

> [A] lot of language has to do with sharing those things around us … we create community with other people as we speak, and it is an abstract community if you like, or at least a verbal community, because it's in another realm than the material community that we're living in our physical environment, and that is important because … in economic so-called communication, we communicate in order **to not share**. We communicate in order for each of us to get our own and not share it with the other person.[8]

Petrilli believes that we create a different kind of human relationship when we're communicating in a gift economy way, an idea that is backed by 'gift economy coach' Selene Aswell, who describes a more relational communication in '*the gift of our listening*'.[9] Aswell, Petrilli and Vaughan all link this gift of communication with a 'maternal' or 'matriarchal' configuration. This is because they note it has a universal resonance, being an experienced typically all infants engage in with their mother or 'motherer', whatever their gender, an almost primal way of interacting with other humans and even non-humans, which has the potential to bring forth a commoning ethos to all relationships, whereby '*gifts of communication enable the flow of other gifts*'.[10,11]

Aswell explains that nurturing and genuine, 'non-violent' communication, also has broader cultural meaning:

> One of the impacts of living in a patriarchal society is that we kind of get a bit more numb to the needs around us. We get a bit more numb to the expression of needs that are constantly happening [and] I think that we can say that the same thing is happening with the planet, where the expression of needs is escalating in volume until we can't ignore it….[12]

With the category of 'non-material gift requests' easily the most prevalent activity on the GKNs, it was clear that the GKE model, with its purposeful exclusion of transaction and currency, did encouraged genuine communications around problem sharing. The model enabled members to express personal vulnerabilities in expectation of a being both heard and responded too 'in kind', whatever their gender:[13]

> We moved to Melbourne at the beginning of the pandemic with our toddler and so we haven't got to meet other parents. Playgrounds are open but we want to avoid crowds to minimize the chance of catching covid. It's really hard to see our little boy unable to interact with other kids though … Is anyone else in a similar situation and maybe wants to meet in a safe way? Please message.
> 7 comments, 15 reactions

> I live alone and this lockdown is getting so hard. The sadness is crippling and I am wondering if anyone knows whether friends and relatives are allowed to visit me to provide social support under caregiving rules? Thanks
> 53 comments, 20 reactions

With all 764 'COVID keyword-responsive' posts having fitted into one or more of the gift economy categories created, I then sought to establish whether the GKE model encompassed the core tenets of a degrowth, gift economy.

Open Localisation

To test whether the GKE model, and the economic behaviours of members might be considered an example of degrowth, the 2020 book *Exploring Degrowth* by Anitra Nelson and Vincent Liegey proved a useful benchmark.

In seeking to define degrowth, the authors describe four core values: 'frugal abundance', 'conviviality', 'open relocalisation' and the 'decolonising of the growth imaginary'.[14]

The first of these, 'open relocalisation', or 'open localism' as it is also referred to, argues for the limitation of both global and national economies, to instead concentrate on local production, local provisioning and responding to local need.

François Schneider explains how the degrowth-archetype of localism differs from localised governance models such as those which are seeking to establish ethnic separatism, to instead function as:

> A distancing from closure, with an openness that is not about top-down universalism: not about generalizing the reign of individual profit, but neither the vision of a world made of cultural clusters.[15]

In other words, the degrowth tenet of open localism is distinct from 'tribalistic' formations which might tacitly imply a sense of (racial) purity or other inherent difference, offering instead an *open culture* which both communicates and engages in trade with neighbouring groups and/or clans, and yet remains anchored to localised collective provisioning.

Considering the GKE model in this context of open (re)localisation during the pandemic, seemed to reveal a strong alignment. Although GKNs are clearly not the representative and participatory democracies conceived by theorists such as Terry Leahy and Tim Hollo, each of the GKNs explored in my research exhibited both an ethos and a practice of open localism, welcoming newcomers to the group/area, responding to the needs of others, and routinely recycling local produce and materials.

A Renewed Sense of Place

Newly cognisant of the physical environs of their 'locked down' community, members of the virtual neighbourhoods of the GKNs often exhibited a new, or renewed, sense of place. There was also much evidence of a sense of connection to others living in the same area, even though it was evident very few members knew each other outside of the virtual community.

This sense of communal experience was expressed, for example, in posts focused on the provisioning of hard-to-get material goods. It was also recorded in the significant number of posts either requesting, or provisioning, locally focused information and in 'non-material gift' posts, where members expressed a new messages of appreciation for their physical location and its natural environment. The communal experience of the pandemic lockdowns seemed to drive a sense of openness and an unexpected willingness to respond to the needs of other members. It also created a sense of belonging, or of being part of a connected community, as responses to the August 2020 member survey reveal. Here:

- 89% of members agreed their GKN increased their sense of belonging to their community;[16]
- 78.9% of members visited/read posts on their GKN daily, on average;
- 74% rated their GKN '8 out of 10 or higher' for helping them to solve problems;
- 34% stated their GKN had been very 'extremely helpful' in helping them to solve problems;
- 66% stated that their GKN had 'empowered them to ask for help'; and
- 91% agreed that their GKN had driven positive outcomes for the local community.

The 2020 survey showed that a majority of those surveyed—82.5%—were new to their Network, most involved for less than 2 years. Although not directly asked about the role of COVID and attendant lockdowns in prompting them to join, it seems likely that the enforced localisation of human life played a significant role. In addition, over *one quarter* (28%) reported that their membership had resulted in face-to-face, i.e., offline, social interactions with other members.

While the GKNs are not designed to enable or incorporate the sort of collective decision-making and processes of local production that would be seen in any fully realised degrowth 'open relocalisation', the virtual community model did show significant patterns in the commoning of both goods and resources during COVID (lockdowns in particular), even if these exchanges, unlike a true degrowth model, took place within the macro growth economy.

So although not the fully-fledged 'open relocalisation' of degrowth, the GKNs nevertheless clearly encouraged, even activated degrowth and/or gift economy behaviours; characteristics of an 'economy oriented around needs not money, profit, debts and growth'.[17]

Requests for support or advice were often responded to with a 'hive mind' approach to problem-solving, as the GKN case study below shows (see Fig. 6.2).

AUTHOR: *Hi everyone I am taking a mental health break and wondering if anyone can donate any clothes or craft stuff please, as I can't have any visitors...*

22 reactions and 84 comments

> **AZ**: *I might. What type of craft things are you allowed?*

AUTHOR: *Most things are ok, thank you*

> **AZ**: *I will have a look tomorrow... Just wanted to say, thoughts are with you* ❤️

> **MM**: *Good on you for working on your mental health. I've been in your shoes and know the feeling* ❤️

AUTHOR: *Thank you I'm doing it for my family and also. hoping it'll help me. Lol*

> **SB**: 💜 *I can't make it there personally but can mail you some things* 😑 *I have also experienced a psyche ward...Take care* 💜

AUTHOR: *Thanks so much! So hard coming in with all the restrictions* 😞

> **SB**: *Bad timing but it would be challenging regardless.*

> **RT**: *I see a visit a psychiatrist too and would 100% love to help you if I lived closer. I hope other GKN members can!*

> **CP**: *I relate; You've had a rough trot! Meds are such trial and error... incredulous in this day and age but there will be the right one found for you. Each is a lesson about what does or doesn't work – it's taken 4 years for me of hospitalisations, and various therapies. Focusing on lifestyle helps.*

AUTHOR: *You've been through an experience like me - too much trial and error! I really hope I get a great doctor. I'm lucky to have a supportive family too xx*

> **JB**: *As a peer, it doesn't sound like your treating team is a good match? That's really hard...To be pragmatic maybe just take what you trust and question the rest. Asking hard questions can be fruitful but can be so hard! You can also ask for a second opinion or different psychologists. The nurse manager can be helpful person to speak with... thinking of you.*

AUTHOR: *I'm not confident but I'll try talking to the nurse.*

> **JB**: *I'm not confident either but it was worth it for me as my team were making me feel worse. No pressure to change. You can always do it a bit at a time and see how you feel.*

> **BL**: *I live nearby so will go through my wardrobe and maybe drop off tomorrow afternoon?*

AUTHOR: I really appreciate that!

Fig. 6.2 Example: The collective decision-making and provisioning of the 'hive mind'. (Note, this example relates to no single author, but is a pastiche of GKN exchanges typical during the pandemic.)

ZD: *I have wool that I could drop to a friend in the area?*

WL: *I live around the corner and can drop some crochet things and art supplies at reception.*

AW: *Well done girl for getting support* ❤️

ST: *Be kind to yourself and be proud of you!*

BD: *You are trying to stay positive and do your best. I was going thru a rough time and started doing a dance workout - you can join me if interested. It's super easy and fun*

CB: *It is such a tough time, I'm thinking of you! You're not within my 5km zone but I have a friend nearby and could give her some craft things for you?*

AUTHOR: *I just wanted to thank you all sooo much for the kind and generous support from this group! It's meant soo much and I hope I can repay you somehow when I'm better.*

[LATER] AUTHOR: *I'm home! I just wanted to thank you all soo very much for the wonderful comments, gifts, and messages…I'm humbled and grateful for this community of love.* 🙂 🙂

Fig. 6.2 (continued)

Free of Judgement

With the concept of 'open localism' effectively rejecting the exclusive and hierarchical spaces of neoliberal capitalism, it was notable that interactions on the GKNs seemed to be much more other-focused than the ego-centric 'blame cultures' of the paid pandemic workplace; cultures where 'the reign of individual profit' dominated.[18]

The openness of the GKNs was conveyed by survey respondents in both explicit and tacit expressions relating to inclusion:

- People respond in a way that is welcoming and free of judgement;
- Helps me understand people in my neighbourhood;
- Never any judgement or anger and always support;
- As a single mum away from my home it's nice to have a place to ask for help;
- It is a very inclusive place, and everyone is helpful;
- The community comes together to support each other no matter who they are;

- Mid-40s with young baby, homeless and with nothing. Moved to public housing and despite our circumstances, GKN members have accepted us for who we are, not what we don't have. It's reignited my belief in the human race;
- Just a feeling of comfort in such a caring, inclusive community, all willing to help each other;
- My world seems brighter and more positive when I see posts of help wanted and support provided. I don't know these people but feel they are my people.[19]

Frugal Abundance

The second tenet of degrowth from Liegey and Nelson is that of 'frugal abundance'. This explicitly relates to living within the finite resources of the planet; however the word 'frugal' also articulates a moral alternative to the excesses of consumer capitalism; defying notions of *'scarcity'* purposely constructed by growth capitalism through a 'debt-based' money system which 'relies on fear and scarcity to maintain its value and power'.[20]

As an economic/social paradigm which is highly parasitic on slave labour/wages from the global South, and increasingly, although to a much lesser extent, workers in the global North; this conception of frugal abundance works to both challenge the extractivist practices of the growth paradigm as well as broader settings of excess. Similarly, the use of the word 'abundance', may suggest some alignment with the material luxuries of capitalism, but in fact describes the very different and largely unquantifiable richness which sits at the heart of collective provisioning and a relational commoning of care.

Considering the GKNs through this lens of frugal abundance, we see direct alignment with the GKE 'vision', which states a central purpose of 'creating connected, healthy and sustainable communities by facilitating compassionate human engagement and collaboration'.[21] This precept of frugal abundance is also reflected in what members said about their motivation for using the Networks:

In the 2020 GKE survey (of 3402 members) for example, 69% of respondents stated their reason for engaging with their GKN page/newsfeed, was to share—*to gift*—'free items'. By 2022, this number had risen *inordinately* to 81%.

Conviviality

While the COVID crisis and associated economic measures were epitomised by a polarity of opinion in Australia, as in most other countries, the white noise of mainstream and social media didn't appear to pervade the Good Karma Networks, which generally espoused a very different sort of *social equivalence*: a *conviviality* that Nelson, Liegey and other degrowth activists align with degrowth practice.

This conviviality was partly 'designed in', with a key function of the Administrator ('Guardian') role being to monitor posts and comments to ensure they comply with the central GKE tenet of 'positivity'. While this stress on positivity was not without controversy, as I will discuss later, the three networks observed over the pandemic period seemed to function largely without controversy, and with a strong and clear conviviality, a reproduction of the social glue.

In addition to sharing material items, practices within these micro gift economies typically also included humorous and self-deprecating stories, and, as noted earlier, responding to others in non-judgemental and care-full ways. The commonality of expressions of shared interests/concerns and of a group 'identity' were markedly different to the individualistic and competitive quid pro quo exchanges described by women workers in the corporatised care sectors of the pandemic, where 52% of women had reported experiences of workplace bullying or bullying workplace cultures.

By contrast, the convivial environments of the GKNs offered customary expressions of community cohesion and solidarity, some of which would sometimes even spill into real life.

'Economic' activities taking place on the Networks over the COVID period seem to suggest that instead of *pride*, or any expectation of quid pro quo reciprocity, that gift-giving and the receiving of gifts on the Networks were essentially *non-transactional*. The survey comments show that users felt able to reach out should they need to; however, more attention was awarded *to the feelings that arose* from reading interactions between others, exchanges which expressed help and saw gifts of advice, care and/or material goods freely and warmly given.

That people would go out of their way to contribute support and care to strangers, and without expectation of immediate or even deferred trade off, seemed more aligned with human sentiment that was *other-oriented*.

Carmen's case study is a typical example (see Fig. 6.3).

Carmen's Story

Carmen had been a member of her local GKN prior to the pandemic. When 2020 brought economic downturn, she and her husband were immediately affected. While Carmen was eligible for JobKeeper, her partner became unemployed. With three children at home and 'not able to go anywhere, or do anything', it was an uncertain time. The family 'didn't want to spend money, but we needed things.'

Living with her immediate family, Carmen didn't experience the isolation from community that many were experiencing, but the pandemic still brought significant challenges. With her usual volunteering at an animal sanctuary and at an aged care facility both suspended, Carmen found her GKN not only offered a distraction, but also offered a sense of a relationship to, and within, her local community.

'You want to give...but particularly to your neighbourhood, perhaps to someone who lives in your street and needs support.' Carmen realised that most people wouldn't want to 'ask for charity' or 'feel they have to have to beg for something they need... I saw a post on another network about giving and receiving, and so I shared it with GKN.'

<u>**Carmen:**</u> ***What is something you can't afford but need? □ Maybe you have something and can pass it on? I saw this post on another group & it was amazing to see the kindness and generosity at this time of year so let's carry it on! No selling; this is a giving post! Maybe we can help each other... □***

33 reactions/140 comments[5]

SS: *I need no gap fee telehealth with a EMDR or TRTP therapist...*

MB: *EMDR has a $100 fee but this private insurance may cover it* [shares link].

MA: *I've done EMDR at* [shares link]. *Don't recommend it on Telehealth. It's an inpatient program. It would be 18k without insurance so look into what funds will cover it.*

CN: *I'd never heard of these types of therapies... Is one better than another?*

BB: *EMDR is better when face to face than telehealth because there's assessment before. Government funds some services*

MA: *Ask your doctor about a mental health plan.*

MB: *There's still a $100 fee for EMDR* 😕

KH: *Ridiculous the mental health plan doesn't cover this. My appointments were $200 with only $50 rebate. I couldn't afford it.*

SP: *I'm an EMDR therapist and work via telehealth. Many of my clients prefer online. You do have to pay a gap fee but if anyone wants any info I'm happy to chat. SW, sorry you're*

Fig. 6.3 Case study, Carmen. (The comments/responses have been deidentified and condensed, but retain the intention of the writer.)

not making progress. It can be hard to find the right services.

SW: *Can you spare a chat? I'll PM my mobile number. Thanks*

SW *to CN: Both recommended. TRTP is from Australia and I've seen people change over 4-8 sessions*

CN: *I'll do more research. Thank you!* 😊

SW *to KH: I wasted a visit because I didn't ask about bulk billing*

SW: *MA, I would love to hear more! Have a great weekend.*

SP: *Sure SW, happy to chat. Let's PM* 😊

LC: I need to spot clean a 7 seater couch and mattresses. 😔 **4 kids and dogs!**

BL: *LO, I have a brand new Spot Clean, you are welcome to my old one. It's still working perfectly.*

LC: *Yes please, I'll pm you!!*

PG: In desperate need of a lawn mower; can't afford one...

FB: *PG, I have a petrol lawnmower but it's in need of a service; if you'd like it.*

PG: *FB, Thankyou that would be wonderful...*

CC: *We have a petrol whipper snipper you are welcome to. PM me if interested.*

PG: *That sounds wonderful ...yes please! Pm sent.*

Fig. 6.3 (continued)

In a similar way, gifts of unpaid care and support typical to the GKNs, seemed to evidence a form of 'community reproduction' that was open and inclusive, more focused on shared identity and reciprocity, as explicit in degrowth theories or 'imaginaries', and very different to the processes of mobbing, exclusion and gaslighting in the growth economy:

> Hi Community, I hope you are all doing well? I am writing because I have just started to transition my gender during COVID. It's been pretty hard because I have to sew so that I can have clothes that are right. The body dysphoria that I experienced before this journey nearly ended me. I'm won-

dering if anyone might have a dressmaker's mannequin or fabric that they no longer need? I'm on a pension and can't afford to buy anything. Pick up will be complicated as I have disability and will need to organise support. Thank you for reading this!

102 reactions/90 comments[22]

The Gift of Time

A defining difference between the two economic models presented in this book, that of 'pandemic capitalism' and the second a degrowth example, is the *gift of time*. If the toxic workplaces in the 'business of care' were conspicuous for their extreme workload pressures, duties outside of the job description and a sense of workers feeling either bullied, or left alone to manage the barely manageable, the GKNs instead showed how work, or a 'workplace' outside of the time-bound transactionalism of paid employment, could actively drive convivial behaviours.

With time repeatedly pronounced the 'profound' and 'greatest gift' of the early pandemic, the sudden slowing of hustle culture led to genuine expressions of appreciation for a world beyond growth, a deeper appreciation of family time and slow tasks of subsistence such as baking.[23,24,25]

While commuter hustle has fully returned to Australian cities in 2023, it is notable that 85% of 2022 survey respondents selected '*sharing humour, gratitude and other positive experiences*' as the activity they found 'most beneficial' in their involvement with the GKNs, activities which generally *take time*, and which were notably absent in the paid workplaces of the pandemic frontline:

> Hello Karmites! Is anyone missing a bag of doughnuts? About a month ago, I found 2 packs on my doorstep which I thought was an accidental addition to my groceries delivered the day before. I left them on the front gate but no one has claimed then. I thought it was just a weird one off but then yesterday I had another mystery delivery… So, is anyone missing doughnuts? Or maybe this is some weird initiation ritual for me lol?[26]
>
> 40 comments/125 reactions

Care-full

In 2020, the Feminisms and Degrowth Alliance (FaDA), wrote of its hope that the pandemic would inspire a shift away from growth capitalism towards a more 'care-full' model of civilisation.[27] While the GKE model is not without criticism, as we shall see, occasional instances of 'bad karma' were outweighed by a commonality of appreciation of the GKE model's emphasis on reciprocity, care*gifting* and positive exchanges of care and support:

- So much gratitude is expressed on this site and people reach out to each other;
- I don't like asking for help, but the care and generosity of members is life enhancing;
- It's the best village mentality; everyone wants to care;
- A safe place to ask for assistance or recommendations;
- It connects people who have to those who need; and those who need help, to those that can give help;
- It's just a feeling of comfort that this is such a caring, inclusive community;
- I feel blessed to live amongst so many good people … It restores my faith in humanity seeing lovely things posted or when people are helping people out of the goodness of their hearts. It makes me safe and happy;
- Nice to know I can reach out if needed;
- I am part of a community that is reliable with help, support, connection and care;
- I've never before lived in a neighbourhood that is so open to helping others;
- Immediate responses to my questions by caring people;
- So much generosity, kindness and support.[28]

As gift economy advocate Peggy Antrobus describes, when talking about how (colonial) capitalism continues to shape Caribbean cultures:

> [W]e have drawn more and more into this notion that the market is the only thing…drawn more and more into the idea that we must commoditize everything, that everything must have a price … Gift economy reminds us of the existence and the power of another kind of economy.[29]

While the workplaces of *Generation Expendable?*—wholly situated within the growth paradigm—drove worker competition, individualisation and toxic interpersonal relations, in sharp contrast, the unpaid workspaces of the Good Karma model, sitting broadly outside of historical and patriarchal economic structures, suggest that real values (can) still define Australian community life; if we just organise in ways which support them.

In This Chapter …

In this chapter, we have seen how the GKNs functioned as an alternative and convivial care workplace during the pandemic. For Australian's living under strict lockdowns, the need for locally-focused goods, support and information was pressing. The GKNs offered members care without judgement, and within a context of conviviality and openness.

In contrast, the pandemic 'businesses of care' were characterised by extreme workloads, pressure and even bullying and unsafe work environments. For women in paid employment, there was often little time to nurture the caring and reciprocal relationships that were seen to have developed in the unpaid care workplace.

In the Next Chapter …

I will present further evidence of activities on the GKNs during 2021 and 2021, to test my hypothesis that these hyper-local virtual spaces comprised a degrowth or 'gift economy' during the pandemic, and looking forward, whether they offer a potential template of alternatives to growth capitalism.

Notes

1. Craig, L., & Churchill, B. (2021). Working and caring at home: Gender differences in the effects of COVID-19 on paid and unpaid labor in Australia. *Feminist economics*, *27*(1–2), 310–326.
2. Miles, A. (2004). Women's Giving: A New Frame for Feminist Policy Demands. A Radically Different World View Is Possible. The Gift Economy Inside and Outside of Patriarchal Capitalism conference. Nov 12–14, 2004. Audio transcript: http://gift-economy.com/a-radically-different-world-view-is-possible/. Accessed Nov 2022.
3. Cinelli, M., Quattrociocchi, W., Galeazzi, A., Valensise, C. M., Brugnoli, E., Schmidt, A. L., ... & Scala, A. (2020). The COVID-19 social media infodemic. *Scientific reports*, *10*(1), 1–10.
4. Vaughan, G. (2023). The Gift of Communication. Maternal Gift Economy Salon #37. https://www.maternalgifteconomymovement.org/salon-37-the-gift-of-communication/. Accessed Jan 2023.
5. Vaughan, G. (2023). Ibid.

6. Vaughan, G. (2023). Ibid.
7. Petrilli, S. (2023). The Gift of Communication. Maternal Gift Economy Salon #37. https://www.maternalgifteconomymovement.org/salon-37-the-gift-of-communication/. Accessed Jan 2023.
8. Petrilli, S. (2023). Ibid.
9. Aswell, S. (2023). The Gift of Communication. Maternal Gift Economy Salon #37. https://www.maternalgifteconomymovement.org/salon-37-the-gift-of-communication/. Accessed Jan 2023.
10. Aswell, S. (2023). Ibid.
11. The concept of a gift economy model as perhaps 'maternal' or female-coded is examined in later chapters. I introduce it here only to provide further context for the research methodology.
12. Aswell, S. (2023). Ibid.
13. All quotes from the GKNs are a pastiche of common interactions/exchanges during COVID, to ensure users are not directly identifiable.
14. Liegey, V. & Nelson, A. (2020). Exploring Degrowth. Reproduced in Pluto Books Blog: https://www.plutobooks.com/blog/the-four-principles-of-degrowth/. Accessed Feb 2021.
15. Quote indirectly attributed to François Schneider, Degrowth Summer School blurb.https://summerschool.degrowth.org/2015/06/04/degrowth-and-open-localisation/. Accessed March 2023.
16. Across all 36 Good Karma Networks.
17. Liegey, V. & Nelson, A. (2020). Exploring Degrowth. Reproduced in Pluto Books Blog: https://www.plutobooks.com/blog/the-four-principles-of-degrowth/. Accessed Feb 2021.
18. Schneider, F. (2015). Degrowth and Open-Localisation. Degrowth Summer School Blurb. https://summerschool.degrowth.org/2015/06/04/degrowth-and-open-localisation/. Accessed Nov 2021. Accessed June 2019.
19. The Good Karma Effect (2023). Unpublished data from the Good Karma Effect Member Survey 2022.
20. Brouillet, C. (2007). Women and the Gift Economy. A radically different World view is possible. Vaughan, G. (Ed). (2007). Inanna Publications. p. 196. Accessed June 2021.
21. The Good Karma Effect. Published online at: https://www.goodkarmaeffect.com/about/good-karma-effect. Accessed Nov 2022.
22. This example is a pastiche of a number of exchanges which occurred in across the GKNs during the pandemic and relates to no one individual.
23. Marr, M. (2020). https://www.phillyburbs.com/story/opinion/columns/more-voices/2020/05/19/guest-opinion-appreciating-gift-time/1183028007/. Guest Opinion: Appreciating the gift of time in the quiet of the COVID-19 pandemic. Accessed June 2021.

24. Telep, P. (2020). University of Central Florida. Some Don't Realize What a Profound Gift of Time This Pandemic Is. *UCF Today*, July 29, 2020. Accessed June 2021.
25. Lacicha, I. (2020). Here's why time is the greatest gift during this pandemic. CEBU Daily. Nov 10, 2020. https://cebudailynews.inquirer.net/350006/heres-why-time-is-the-greatest-gift-during-this-pandemic. Accessed June 2021.
26. This example is a pastiche of a number of exchanges which occurred in across the GKNs during the pandemic and relates to no one individual.
27. Feminisms and Degrowth Alliance (FaDA). (2020). Collaborative Feminist Degrowth: Pandemic as an Opening for a Care-Full Radical Transformation. Degrowth.de, May 8, 2020. Accessed June 2020.
28. The Good Karma Effect (2023). Unpublished data from the Good Karma Effect Member Surveys 2020 and 2022.
29. Antrobus, P. (2004). A Radically Different World View Is Possible: The Gift Economy Inside and Outside of Patriarchal Capitalism conference, November 12–14, 2004. http://gift-economy.com/the-gift-economy-inside-and-outside-patriarchal-capitalism-part-4/. Accessed June 2021.

CHAPTER 7

The Unbearable Hazard of Hierarchy

Abstract As 'society' is increasingly substituted by 'economy' in the twenty-first century, transactionalism permeates Australia's institutions and workplaces, as it does across much of the globe. What has been described as 'the commodification of everything' presents the notion of an ego-focused quid pro quo or individualised profitmaking as normal behaviour, an 'exchange logic' that degrowth and gift economy scholars tell us must be challenged if we are to meaningfully address the polycrises of late-stage capitalism and economic fundamentalism. With 'the gift paradigm' offering a potential alternative to the discourse of growth economics, this chapter relates survey findings and case studies from *The Gift Highway* study, arguing that the repeated practice of gifting behaviours brings both individual and collective good. The author does however single out issues which, even in the gift economy model examined, can still emerge wherever a structural power dynamic remains unchecked.

Keywords Hierarchy • Gift economy • Reciprocity • Degrowth • Exchange economy • Women • Gender • Care • Hyper-local • Virtual

M. Jordan, *Women's Work in the Pandemic Economy*,
https://doi.org/10.1007/978-3-031-40154-1_7

Introduction

Diversity, inclusion, and equity policies may now be broadly endorsed in Australian organisations, yet research shows that 'not all diversities are equal'. Even within government, hierarchies of value endure. For example, while there may be greater overall gender and racial equality, 'social class is ignored, and people with invisible, subtle, or complex diversities are seldom considered.'[1]

With 'society' now replaced by 'economy', we see a culture of transactionalism permeate both public and private spheres, an 'exchange logic' driving 'the commodification of everything' through 'rational' economic behaviours of exchange equivalence.[2,3,4]

In the highly stressed and feminised workplaces of care capitalism, with staff routinely expected to shoulder a significant workload, workers may expect fairness in the division of work and even an 'equal' say—any say—in how things are run. Yet these expectations are diametrically opposed to typical work settings, where workers are overburdened, including with mundane or uncoordinated tasks as we shall see later. Many are also, conversely, underutilised in terms of their skills.[5]

In the workplaces of twenty-first century neoliberal fundamentalism, it is little wonder that workers take a stance of competition and comparison. If a colleague is thought to be doing less, or conversely, to be *doing much better*; resentments and even exclusion may seem the 'logical' response. Taking time to communicate around a mutual division of labour, to mentor, or to encourage professional 'upskilling', activities they are sometimes described as more 'circular', or female-coded work processes, are fundamentally designed out.

When we also consider that many women finish their paid workday only to commence 'the second shift' of unpaid work in the home, another workplace where they may also have subordinate power, we can perhaps understand how bullying behaviours between women become tactical and even *logical*: why workplace bullying is 'always the result of unequal power' and typically 'has a gender dimension'.[6,7]

The Gift Alternative

For gift economy advocate Genevieve Vaughan, the 'gift paradigm' is the antithesis of capitalism's 'logic of exchange'.

Vaughan explains:

> Other societies have been based on gift giving without this strong underlying logic of exchange. In a context where the exchange logic is lacking, or at least not dominant, human interactions can take on an entirely different character. So that even when giving is reciprocated, it is not immediately placed in a framework of exchange, with all the consequences that framework entails, but it remains within a gift paradigm.[8]

As noted earlier, removing currency is one tactic for subverting, and perhaps even overturning, the transactional logic of capitalism. While this is important, it may not however sufficiently address the other functioning dynamism of capitalism: that of *power*.

As we saw in the ubiquity of toxic work cultures in *Generation Expendable?* and in labour market research more broadly, rigidly hierarchical organisational structures are known to drive poor and even dangerous work conditions. Even when 'horizontal' and supposedly 'consumer-centred' decision-making structures are in place, any collective power is nevertheless 'negatively impacted by organisationally privileged actors in governments and bureaucracies.'[9]

The horizontal and collective decision-making championed by degrowth activists seeks to construct, or perhaps reproduce, the systems and cultures of Indigenous and pre-modern gift economies; forms of social organisation which negate capitalism's exchange logic and replace it, as we see in the example of the GKNs, with values of commoning and mutuality, conviviality and reciprocity.

However, even decommodified 'pathways out of capitalism' do not automatically address power imbalances; what I think of as the unbearable hazard of hierarchy, as the following stories show.

Bad Karma

As detailed earlier, the interactions on the Good Karma Networks during COVID had shown evidence of lateral and synergetic decision-making: the hive mind at work. Even if members weren't always troubleshooting problems 'as one', they were still ebbing and flowing in responding collectively to requests for help and routinely engaging in considered and thoughtful discussions with other members.

With dialogue on the platforms being open and transparent, and with engagement wholly voluntary, the collective nature/structure of the communities seemed to act as a sort of self-correcting mechanism wherever ego-oriented exchanges did emerge. Additionally, the 'guardian' moderator was always present in the background, functioning to preserve *community* over *individual.*

As Anitra Nelson envisages in her 2022 book, without money as an organising principle, the 'real values' of care and subsistence are were seen to emerge and even thrive in the GKNs. Disavowing currency and trade of any sort, the exchange logic of *Generation Expendable?* workers seemed wholly absent in the interactions of women workers in *The Gift Highway.* Instead, the GKNs had been configured in a way which clearly encouraged conviviality and reciprocity, where one good deed could often be seen prompting another, and then another, in a very different sort of *economic heuristics* than that of the market. Here, the 'reward' from gifting, or from receiving, seemed mainly to be the prompting of further gifting behaviours from members.

The GKE model is not entirely without hierarchy, however. As with any power imbalance, the single 'guardian' tier occasionally caused problems. With each network typically having only two to three voluntary administrators, this 'power over', as with the hierarchies of the paid workplace, could also encourage expressions of top-down power, as Sandra's story shows (see Fig. 7.1).

In addition to Sandra's experience, another demonstration of 'bad karma' was seen in the 2021 collapse of the Brunswick Good Karma Network, following 'allegations of "toxic positivity", overzealous censorship and racism'.[10]

In this example, problems arose when members of the 23,000-strong group took issue with guardians 'deleting posts about crimes in Brunswick, allegations about a racist assault and the outing of a resident as an alleged neo-Nazi.'[11] Members told journalists they had been evicted from the Network for 'innocuous comments and use of negative emojis'.

In an incident not so dissimilar to the mobbing formations of paid workplaces, the conflict leaked into the 'real world', with photographs of the site's moderators posted on local street poles along with negative commentary.

Good Karma Effect CEO Amy Churchouse told *The Age* newspaper that 'numerous attempts' had been made to resolve the issue but had been ignored: 'We've got a bunch of volunteers who have been trying to keep this community safe and positive, not feeling safe in their own suburb because somebody decided to scream racism from the rooftops.'[12]

Within days, moderators announced the network was going 'into hiatus' and in 2023, a rival 'Brunswick Fairly Good Karma Network', which allows 'some political discussion' boasts over 14,000 members.

Sandra's Story

I moved to [suburb] *just before the pandemic and my girlfriend told me about the local GKN. I said, What's that? She said, You're gonna love it.*

Straightway I felt a sense of camaraderie. The Network very much became a lifeline for me in the pandemic because I was really worried about everything.

As someone in the Arts, I had lost all my work and it felt like the Morrison government just didn't care about the Arts or Artists.

It was a terrible, terrible situation; people even took their lives. I was so lonely and lost.

I do 12 Step recovery, and during COVID I would attend two online meetings every day, just because it was the only contact I was having. Eventually I put up a post on XGKN saying, I've got covid.

I was asking for lemons mainly, but I had people dropping around soup and green smoothies.... It was amazing. I was brought to tears by the kindness, it was so lovely.

Later, I posted about wanting to do the 'Oxfam 100 kilometer' walk; I was looking for a walking partner to do 3 kilometers a day for 30 days. XXXXX responded straightaway with, I'm in.

I did think, What will we talk about? Oh my God, what if we get bored? But from day one we just started walking and never stopped - we had an instant connection and since then we've developed this extraordinary sisterhood. I'm just so grateful.

The XGKN was a massive part of my life during the pandemic; but the sad part is – well, any network has problems, but I soon discovered that the Admins for my particular group were problematic.

One afternoon I had gone through some boxes; all this stuff left over from my marriage which I put up for grabs [on the XGKN page]. But I then got an email from Admin telling me, You're supposed to put it all up on ***one*** *post, not separate. I explained, I'm neurodivergent, I don't know how to do that. And she said, Well, you've got to do it* ***right****. It was just bully, bully, bully.*

Later, they actually banned me for 28 days. This was because my friend had posted about someone leaving a dog in their car on a really hot day. She had put a pic up on the Network and written: Please, don't leave dogs in hot cars. Lots of members were commenting and agreeing. Then all of a sudden, the post was taken down.

So I wrote: Could someone please help me understand why the post about dogs in hot cars has been removed?

And I get a direct message from Admin saying: You don't have the right to discuss this on the public page . You have to deal with us directly.

I said: Why are you talking to me like this? We're all adults. You don't have to use bullying language. They then put a ban on me posting for 28 days. They were absolute bullies.

I'd set up an arrangement with a shoe repair guy, whose shop had closed during COVID. I'd offered my place as a drop off site. He would pick the shoes every Friday and then drop them back, repaired.

Fig. 7.1 Case study: Sandra

It worked really well for about three months. So when I got back after the ban, I put up a post about the shoes and another friend had commented using my name. Straightaway, she receives a direct message from Admin saying: You let [Sandra] on this page, how dare you?!

She replied: I'm not an admin. I don't even know how to [let someone become a member].
The Admin said: Well you must know her? She told them: I cannot stand this sort of harassment.

She then actually decided to leave the group. It was devastating, because the idea is just wonderful, but whoever has the control, has ultimate power. I loved the concept, but the control element permeated the Group Admins; they are truly brutal bullies.

People said to me privately, My God, I'm so scared of the admins. But I really love the group and I don't wanna leave...

I once put up a post saying: I'm getting my coffee delivered this week from XXX and it's free delivery, so if you're thinking of ordering coffee maybe do it now because he's coming to [our neighbourhood] and doesn't charge for delivery. That post was taken down because I was 'promoting a business'.

I complained about what was happening and the way I was treated was appalling - nothing was resolved. So I then spoke to someone on the board and she was wonderful, wanted to see if we could sort it.

I spoke to another friend on the Network who had also been put on a 28 day ban. I asked, what did you do? He said, something really innocuous. I thought, I have to deal with this. I ended up crying on my walks with XXXX until she said, you've got to leave this group; it's gotten too toxic. We laughed, but you know, it hurt me so deeply that I had to remove myself.

My therapist said, You've been working on yourself for 35 years Sandra; you have real clarity and strong recovery. Sometimes you've just gotta walk away.

I said I'm so grateful, I'm really a fan. I love the whole concept... the beautiful people, the extraordinary people, the strengths, the friendships that I've made, and the strength of the friendships...To know that I could say to people, have this, enjoy it, made me happy. Better than stuff gathering dust for years.

I used to love saying, Yes, I've got... whatever it was: I'll leave it on my front porch for you. That notion of giving things away... There's something nice that happens when you get into that practice of giving.

In the 12 step model we say recovery starts at the end of a tea towel. You help set up, do the dishes at the end. You're hanging around with a bunch of alcoholics and talking about stuff. What happens in the GKN is a closed shop. If they don't like you - it's not acceptable behaviour in any workplace, or volunteer organisation. In 12 step models, no one has a position of power for longer than six months. You do the job and then someone else takes it over. I do wonder how often the Admins are rotated because if they don't rotate...well, ultimate power corrupts.

I wrote to the Admins asking, 'help me understand why my posts aren't being approved? And the person said: Well you were rude to me last time. Blah blah blah. I said: What?! You're responding with 15 year old logic. The Admin replied, Well, if you don't like it, just leave. I realise that this 'control' thing is usually a survival trait developed by children in dysfunctional families who then go on to carry that into adult lives, but to just take my posts down and put me on a ban?

Fig. 7.1 (continued)

Being bullied was really devastating because the aim of the GKN is love. When XXXXX and I started walking, we were putting up posts saying, Maybe you could sponsor us? But we were told we weren't allowed unless it was a local charity. You know...rules.

People get caught up. I think that's what happened in that GKN. The Admins were so into control that they lost any sense of humour - some of the things the admins did were seriously insane. It's emotionally exhausting. We're just trying to stay alive and get through the pandemic. We don't have room for petty, bitchy, horrible... You wanna help people shine; offer a helping hand.

How can we share our vulnerability if we feel it has been thrown back at us?

I don't know if it's fixable; as long as there's control at the top, it's never gonna change. We need women like us to shake things up.

Fig. 7.1 (continued)

Toxic Positivity?

The above examples are not to suggest that a gift economy model is just as prone to bullying and aggressively self-centred interactions as the workplaces of paid employment. Rather, that hierarchies of power have an innate propensity to differentiate, and from there, to drive discord through 'me against other' and 'us against them' sentiments.

Whether in paid employment or 'beyond money', hierarchies of power, I suggest, customarily drive dissent.

It is also pertinent that some GKN members found the resolutely positive ethos of the GKE model to be artificial and overly enforced. In the 2022 member survey, we see occasional comments about this 'toxic positivity':

- Policed overzealously, even on posts where there is no possibility of harm;
- Blocked just for saying that I was upset with a post;
- Everything is so politically correct it's ridiculous … moderated within an inch of its life;
- Excessive virtue signalling by members;
- Era of overzealous control by administrators;
- Forced to be toxically positive.[13]

Moderating the Gift Economy

With only a few voluntary moderators overseeing what might be up to 100 posts and responses on the GKNs daily, it wasn't surprising to note some inconsistency across the networks studied. Recommendations for local businesses for example, were common in the 'non-material gifts' categories of two of the GKNs studied and yet rarely seen in the third, suggesting that guardians administrating the latter group imposed stricter parameters than in the other two groups.

That virtual communities have the potential to become 'seething, explosive' had also been observed prior to the Brunswick GKN skirmish noted above.[14] Writing in 2020, journalist Melissa Fyfe describes these types of Facebook groups as '*places for communities to share information, support each other, do good deeds*' but also, '*as harangued moderators can attest*', communities which '*often devolve into something more Lord of the Flies than Pollyanna*.[15] Fyfe observes that, 'If the internet has a class system, moderators sit at the bottom….'

Interestingly, a survey undertaken by the organisation of Australian Community Managers, shows that around three quarters of administrators of online groups are *female*; 68% 'Millennials' who are typically well-educated and yet with half earning 'below Australia's average wage'.[16]

Decolonising the Growth Imaginary

The Gift Highway study revealed that the 'labours' on the GKNs during COVID were highly gendered. Not only had the two GKE surveys shown a more than 85% female membership, but the pandemic interactions across the three Naarm-based networks were also female-dominated.

With *all* the keyword posts identified fitting comfortably into the gift economy indicators used to analyse the data, the research hypothesis of hyper-local virtual communities operating as micro gift economies was clearly demonstrated. However, to what extent might they align with the fourth and final degrowth tenet cited by Nelson and Liegey, that of *decolonising the 'growth imaginary*'?[17,18,19]

The concept of 'decolonisation' is of course co-opted from its original purpose of recognition and redress for hundreds of years of geo-cultural colonisation and European capitalist expansion.[20] While the use of the word decolonise by degrowth advocates has been rightly criticised, the word remains highly effective in conveying the very real and present imperative to liberate our collective imagination from the all-pervasive growth hegemony.

For degrowth advocates, 'decolonising the imaginary' would see a fundamental shift in the way human societies, particularly those of the global North, (don't) think about the destructiveness of capitalism, nor the increasingly urgent climate emergency.[21]

I believe we see some evidence of this 'decolonising', of minds shifting away from exchange economy heuristics, both in the routine nature of women's/member's activities of gift giving and provisioning of care, but also in the collectivist hive mind murmurations of a system of production which sits largely outside of the market. We see this influence upon what I earlier framed as the imagination infrastructure of members in many of the survey comments:

- A real sense of community as opposed to profit making;
- Genuine moments where people see the bigger picture rather than benefiting themselves;
- I know I won't be "sold" something;
- Reminds me that most people are good, want to help and are not out for themselves;
- People are so willing to help, it inspires me;
- Even if people take advantage, the outpour of generosity makes me hopeful that humanity still exists;
- It reminds me of the humanity of strangers;
- Keeps you connected to the place where you live. We are all so busy we neglect the good in our own back yards;
- Community spirit is much alive, so unexpected;
- I love the way locals interact through giving and receiving;
- It shows we are a community, not everyone is just out for themselves.[22]

Overall, the interactions on the three GKNs during the two pandemic years show that, contrary to the cultures of the paid care frontline and growth discourse, and left to mostly self-organise in an alternative economic environment, women workers—indeed GKN members of all genders—adapted easily and automatically to an alternative, gifting or degrowth paradigm.

Reciprocity or Quid Pro Quo?

Reciprocity is a defining feature of both degrowth and gift economy models. Therefore, if we are to move on from capitalism's 'rational economic man' towards a more collective social organisation, *systemic reciprocity* will be essential.

Yet there is an ambiguity, or potential misalignment, between the concepts of reciprocity and exchange economic behaviour.

Homi Bhabha writes about the 'slippage' that can occur in 'the micrologies of power, the diverse enunciative sites of discourse'. Bhabha specifically locates in 'the ambivalence of colonial discourse', the power of words and language in a way not dissimilar to Barbara Alice Mann's highlighting of 'big lie' of patri-colonial capitalism.[23,24] These scholars warn us therefore, that any decolonising of the growth imaginary can be neither concrete nor finite. Rather, that decolonising the growth imaginary must be an ongoing project with routine checks and balances.

We can see the propensity of Bhabha's concept of slippage even in well-evidenced forecasts of how a degrowth world might function. For example, Terry Leahy speculates that in a money-free, gift-based economy '*there's no motive to produce unnecessary stuff. So the motive to produce things for other people is prestige, affection, long-term reciprocity.*[25]

For Leahy, *prestige* would operate as a driver of reciprocal gift-giving:

> What I'd say about the gift economy is that it works not to market demand, but through people's interest in producing things that other people want and will need. In other words, you get prestige and status from producing not just for your own community…the prestige that comes with supplying for a real need in other communities and also the commitment to be part of a production chain that provides for a whole lot of communities.[26]

This notion of prestige or status in the gift economy model was also noted by Marcel Mauss, but other economic thinkers such as Yunxiang Yan, note that it can be problematic.[27,28]

We can see that Leahy's predicted motivations, grounded in an evidence base of traditional gift economies, are not only pragmatic, but probably also realistic. However, this notion of prestige perhaps too closely echoes the transactionalism of our current, ego-oriented exchange capitalism; where status and prestige are a key driver of economic behaviour. A system that 'maternal' gift economy advocates are at pains to call out as essentially 'masculine' in nature. Perhaps a society based so fundamentally upon such a characterisation of reciprocity might too easily tip into the very ego-oriented behaviours that underpin capitalism's greed. Even the good intentions of a gift economy model can, as Madelyn's case study suggests, become blurred in practice (see case study in Fig. 7.2).

It is here then, I would argue, that feminist philosophers advocating for a 'maternal' gift paradigm, or a 'rematriation' of culture offer the most persuasive argument: that any gift paradigm must fundamentally aim to be 'other-oriented' in the way of the motherer, and not *ego-oriented*, as the rational economic actors of the global free market typically are. This other-oriented praxis would recognise the need for any essential hierarchy to be always revolving, cycling beyond one single person or group to a dispersal of power. It would support, I suggest, a genuinely decolonised and reciprocal *imaginary*.

Madelyn's story

Thank you for letting me join this wonderful community group. I'm new to the area and have just had a baby 3 weeks ago. As a single parent and with Covid-19 restrictions etc, my plan for getting to know the new neighbourhood is out the window right now. No mother's groups etc that I had been counting on, and so I was hoping there might be some connections I could make through here to help me feel less isolated. Just online chats obviously for the foreseeable time, but if there's anyone who perhaps has a newborn that would like to connect, a single parent or anyone who might otherwise have some advice and support at the moment I'd be really grateful to form a little local support network, so I don't get too overwhelmed about being just me and baby for the months ahead! Picture for cuteness □

While Madelyn's 'non-material gift request' received 61 reactions and 82 responses from members, including offers of help, social connection and material items, her impression more than two years later was less enthusiastic:

I'm not sure the group is all that helpful. The concept is amazing, but the participants tend to be pretty sanctimonious and patronising. I feel the admin play "parking inspector" but don't know how to manage a group to help people in a dignified way. The help listed on posts rarely eventuates. When compared to a small country town I was in over Christmas, I contracted Covid, and the local community notice board (not GKN) had people leaving supplies like meals and other staples. No big boring comments for all to see, no unsolicited advice, just "here's some provisions and my phone number if you need anything". The GKN seems to be a bit pious by comparison, which I think is down to poor admin choice. It would be amazing to see something like GKN run with less egos, but I can see the challenge with well-meaning but inexperienced volunteers.

Fig. 7.2 Case study: Madelyn, a new single mother

In This Chapter …

We have seen that the Good Karma Effect model encourages caring, convivial and reciprocal relations. However, with human 'economic' behaviour deeply colonised by the values of growth capitalism, the twin logics of competition and individualism may be impossible to entirely structure out. A system of sturdy checks and balances will need to build into any successful post-capitalism, to make sure that power structures do not ever produce, or reproduce, an 'other'.

In the Next Chapter …

I will present further evidence of activities on the GKNs during 2021 and 2021, further testing my hypothesis that these hyper-local virtual spaces comprised a degrowth or 'gift economy' during the pandemic, but also looking forward, to see if they might work at scale, as a real alternative to growth capitalism.

Notes

1. McEwen, C., Pullen, A., Rhodes, C. (2023). It's not all about gender or ethnicity: a blind spot in diversity programs is holding equality back. The Conversation, January 24, 2023. https://theconversation.com/its-not-all-about-gender-or-ethnicity-a-blind-spot-in-diversity-programs-is-holding-equality-back-198237. Accessed Jan 2023.
2. Woman's Day (1987). The Sunday Times Reprint. Epitaph for the eighties? "There is no such thing as society." Brian Deer Investigations Website. https://briandeer.com/social/thatcher-society.htm.
3. Gilbert, J. (2008). Against the commodification of everything: Anti-consumerist cultural studies in the age of ecological crisis. *Cultural studies*, *22*(5), 551–566.
4. Holborow, M. (2018). Language, commodification and labour: The relevance of Marx. *Language* Sciences, 70, 58–67.
5. Baum, S., Bill, A., & Mitchell, W. (2008). Labour underutilisation in metropolitan labour markets in Australia: individual characteristics, personal circumstances and local labour markets. Urban Studies, 45(5–6), 1193–1216.
6. Hutchinson, M., Vickers, M., Jackson, D., & Wilkes, L. (2006). Workplace bullying in nursing: towards a more critical organisational perspective. *Nursing inquiry*, *13*(2), 118–126.

7. Hutchinson, J., & Eveline, J. (2010). Workplace bullying policy in the Australian public sector: why has gender been ignored? *Australian Journal of Public Administration*, *69*(1), 47–60.
8. Vaughan G. (2004). Heterosexual economics: gift giving and exchange. Audio transcript from The Gift Economy Inside and Outside of Patriarchal Capitalism conference. Ottawa, Nov 12–14, 2004. Accessed Nov 2022.
9. Koch, P. (2013). Bringing power back in collective and distributive forms of power in public participation. *Urban Studies*, *50*(14), 2976–2992.
10. O'Neil, P. (2021). Brunswick's Good Karma Network shuts amid claims of 'toxic positivity', racism. The Age, Aug 21, 2021. https://www.theage.com.au/national/victoria/brunswick-s-good-karma-network-shuts-amid-claims-of-toxic-positivity-racism-20210821-p58kq4.html. Accessed Sept 2021.
11. O'Neil, P. (2021). Ibid.
12. O'Neil, P. (2021). Ibid.
13. Good Karma Effect. (2022). Unpublished 2022 Member Survey data.
14. Sackville, K. (2019). Beware the 'seething, explosive' world of feisty Facebook groups. The Age. Feb 26, 2019. https://www.theage.com.au/lifestyle/life-and-relationships/beware-the-seething-explosive-world-of-feisty-facebook-groups-20190226-p51094.html. Accessed May 2022.
15. Fyfe, M. (2020). Social discord: online communities are supposed to bring people together, so why do they often tear us apart? Sydney Morning Herald. May 8, 2020.
16. Australian Community Managers (2020). Survey Results. (Archived version accessed April 2023). https://web.archive.org/web/20210620213253/https://www.australiancommunitymanagers.com.au/research.
17. Decolonising the growth imaginary was originally proposed by French degrowth scholar Serge Latouche. See: Latouche, S. (2018). The path to degrowth for a sustainable society. Factor X: challenges, implementation strategies and examples for a sustainable use of natural resources, 277–284.
18. D'Alisa, G., Demaria, F., and Kallis, G. (Eds). (2015). Imaginary, Decolonisation of in Degrowth, A Vocabulary for a New Era. Routledge.
19. Nelson, A. & Liegey, V. (2020). Exploring Degrowth: A Critical Guide. Pluto Press. Pp 20–48.
20. Deschner, C. & Hursh, E. (2018). Decolonisation and Degrowth. Resilience. Feb 7, 2018. https://www.resilience.org/stories/2018-02-07/decolonisation-and-degrowth/. Accessed May 2022.
21. Asara, V., Profumi, E. and Kallis, G., (2013). Degrowth, democracy and autonomy. Environmental Values, 22(2), pp. 217–239.
22. The Good Karma Effect (2023). Unpublished 2022 Member Survey data.
23. Bhabha, H. K. (2013). Culture's in between. In Multicultural states (pp. 29–36). Routledge.

24. Bhabha, H. K. (1994). Of mimicry and man: The ambivalence of colonial discourse. The location of culture.
25. Leahy, T. (2022). What's Wrong with Money? System Change made Simple. Season 1, Episode 2. https://www.buzzsprout.com/2014361/10918041-what-s-wrong-with-money Audio at Accessed Jan 2023.
26. Leahy, T. (2022). The Gift Economy: Pathways out of Capitalism. System Change made Simple, Season 1, Episode 3 Audio at https://www.buzzsprout.com/2014361/10918058. Accessed Jan 2023.
27. Yan, Y. (2012). The gift and gift economy. In A Handbook of Economic Anthropology, Second Edition. Edward Elgar Publishing.
28. Donlan, W. (1989). The unequal exchange between Glaucus and Diomedes in light of the Homeric gift-economy. *Phoenix*, *43*(1), 1–15.

CHAPTER 8

Economy as a Gender Construct

Abstract This chapter explores what the writer, and other degrowth and feminist advocates believe to be the intrinsically patriarchal nature of capitalism; including how gender and other inequities are reproduced by neoliberal notions of growth, individual liberty and choice, while denying and invisibilising the systemic and structural disadvantage built into the pyramid of capital. The author argues that, just as Australian women are rewarded for adopting a more masculine style of leadership in work settings, a model of 'liberal' or 'corporate' feminism, so too are (Australian) men discouraged and even punished for exhibiting 'female-coded', i.e., caring behaviours. With some theorists linking practices of gift giving to 'maternal' nurture, the 'other-focused' behaviours of 'motherers' towards their children, this chapter considers whether the gift paradigm has the power to challenge capitalism's ego-centred exchange logic.

Keywords Degrowth • Growth • Patriarchy • Capitalism • Collectivism • Gift economy • Masculinity • Gender • Individualism • Masculate • Matriarchy • Rematriation • Maternal • Corporate feminism

M. Jordan, *Women's Work in the Pandemic Economy*,
https://doi.org/10.1007/978-3-031-40154-1_8

Introduction

The cultural myths which underpin how Australians like to see and to present ourselves are pervasive. In modern—neoliberal—incarnations, notions of individual merit and supposedly 'healthy' competition construct and reconstruct the national identity of a 'lucky country', where, as mentioned in the introduction, everybody gets 'a fair go'.

The Australian Cultural Atlas lists the country's 'core concepts' as being:

- Mateship
- Egalitarianism
- Authenticity
- Optimism
- Humility
- Informality
- Easy-going
- Common sense
- Humour[1]

We see these cultural maxims routinely reflected in representations of workplace culture, with hackneyed 'organisational values' espousing 'teamwork' and 'collegiality', while yet remaining structured by rigid workplace hierarchies which expose, or at least, echo the nation's colonial heritage.[2,3,4] It is said that '*Australian values lead to a less competitive workplace environment*'; despite much evidence of high national rates of workplace—and schoolyard—bullying.[5,6] And as noted earlier, the pervasive misogyny identified in our national parliament suggests, as did the findings of *Generation Expendable?*, that Australians may not be as easy-going and 'fair dinkum' as we tell ourselves; and only a good degree of cognitive dissonance lets our imagination infrastructure blind us to patterns of entrenched gender (and racial) inequality.

Economist Leonora Risse explains:

> One way to make sense of how workplaces can feed a culture of the marginalisation and denigration of women is to firstly recognise the ways that workplaces – instead of being the place where we all come together to productively undertake our job duties – can be used by some as a competitive arena for power, status and conquest. Their primary goal is not to "do their job" as per their job description. Their work site, instead, becomes their playpen for another quest. A quest to scale the career ladder, surpass rivals, and claim and

assert authority in the form of seniority of status, privilege and power. And it's a personal quest that is commonly incentivised, legitimised and rewarded by workplace culture itself. Look around at how many workplaces heartily embrace systems of promotions, hierarchies, competitive rankings and special entitlements for seniority, as mechanisms to incentivise performance.[7]

A Gendered Economy

In the context of the gender *binarism* of capital, it is not only men who are valued for displaying hyper-masculine behaviours, *male-coded* behaviours in women workers are also typically rewarded, with masculine constructs of 'rationality' and 'strength', constructs that align with a growth orthodoxy, celebrated, even—particularly—in women workers.

Genevieve Vaughan explains how gender stereotypes are weaponised in the institutions of both work and the family; functioning to uphold and reproduce capitalism:

> We would also need to undo the institutions based on genders constructed in this way to allow all of us to arrive at our true humanity. In fact, it's the institutions that rebroadcast to us all of these paradoxes and this gender construction. Because gender assignments depend not on biology but on the social readings of our biological differences. Women can also be 'not givers' and violent, while men can be nurturing. But the artificial gender norms have been projected into society and taught in homes and schools for centuries.[8]

In the highly corporatised and managerial workplaces of the global North, women, who have fought hard for equal rights, may now be more able to 'climb the ladder' to secure senior positions, yet like men, they must assume 'masculine' characteristics of leadership: what has been described as a 'corporate feminism' or 'girlboss' model, where women workers are rewarded for behaving typically more individualistic, authoritarian, inflexible and *critical of female-coded 'weakness'*.

Leonora Risse summarises this masculine work ethic in women leader as follows:

- Show no weakness;
- Show physical strength and endurance;
- Work comes first;
- Win at all costs.[9]

Men as Gendered

Just as Australian cultural norms reward 'masculine' workplace settings, so too can they punish men who exhibit female-coded behaviours.

We know that binary gender constructs ensure women shoulder the bulk of domestic reproductive work, typically without sufficient recognition and reward. Yet they also function to *masculate* men, again in formations which fundamentally underpin and propel 500-odd years of patri-colonial capitalism.

Vaughan believes this masculation drives the gendered male to uphold the exchange paradigm; also, to both reject and invisibilise the gift giving, 'maternal' economy:

> Before [boys] learn language, they identify with the mother, but then they find they are in a binary opposite category, so they begin to see gift giving as something they must not do … This process which I call masculation is a construction … projected into society at large, into the institutions of society, into the market itself.[10]

For Vaughan:

> Masculated males compete with each other to become the one at the top … However, this is paradoxical … because logically there is only one 'one' at the top. In order to resolve this paradox, multiple hierarchies are established in different areas of life … a categorization process that … is incarnated into a gender stereotype with an agenda of domination [and] projected into our social institutions.[11]

Vaughan's understanding of the male gender as a creation which poses problems at both the individual, and the societal level, is reinforced by Nancy Chodorow's psychoanalytical and sociological analysis of basic sex differences in personality development.

For Chodorow, while it is 'difficult to generalise about the attainment of gender identity and sex-role assumption, since there is such wide variety in the sexual sociology of different societies'; in any given society, 'feminine personality comes to define itself in relation and connection to other people more than masculine personality does.'[12]

Chodorow explains that, in working to achieve a masculine identity which is clearly differentiated from a boy's maternal figure of earlier identification, masculinity is shaped by negative or oppositional approaches.

Both internally, in sense of masculine/gendered self, and externally, as a societal member who 'appropriates to himself and defines as superior particular social activities and cultural (moral, religious and creative) spheres—possibly, in fact, "society" and "culture" themselves.'[13]

Individualism Not Collectivism

The Australian workplaces of late-stage capitalism discourage worker solidarity. Practices of collegiality, and supportive workplace relationships, take time to develop and more time to maintain. Under 30 years of 'new managerialism', a work culture which has been described as 'the organisational arm of neoliberalism', we have seen 'the institutionalising of market principles in the governance of organizations'.

For women workers in the legacy institutions of care and education, 'hierarchical line management … undermine[s] the effective implementation of Equal Employment Opportunity initiatives, as women remain concentrated in the lowest paid and least secure positions.[14,15]

Also in the private sector, echoes of the same formations of hierarchy configured in Australia's colonial/settler past see decision-making typically 'devolved' through linear and cluster-style line management, leaving (typically female) middle managers overseeing operations, supervising staff and having an administrative role. Workload at this intermediate tier of 'bureaucratic managerialism' leaves little room for either strategic, or participatory, decision-making processes.[16,17]

As noted earlier, organisational systems which are highly formalised and hierarchical have a negative effect on organisational performance and quality in healthcare and education settings.[18,19,20] In contrast, research shows that *flat* or horizontal work structures are 'more likely to yield positive results' in healthcare quality.[21,22]

Corporate Feminism and the Girlboss

For women workers in feminised sectors, organisational configurations which might actually encourage team identity, establish processes around the fair division of work, and ensure relationship-centred and collective work practices, have been structured out. This is not only the case in Australia of course, across much of the world, late-stage neoliberalism sees workers rights diminished under ever-increasing workloads, stagnant wages and declining worker wellbeing:[23]

> Capitalist dynamics produce inequities. In terms of enterprises, the carrots and rewards of competition play out as either more or less profits, even bankruptcy, all based on a firm's monetary efficiency. There is more downward pressure on wages the more one is supervised; those most controlled tend to be paid the least. Similarly, at the top of the pecking order, owners and managers tend to put upward pressure to increase.[24]

Like other countries of the global North, Australia has undergone significant deunionisation across the last 40 years. Staffing is increasingly casualised, leaving 'workforces' fragmented as permanent full-time positions give way to temporary and short-term contracts, discouraging collegiality and also a more cooperative workplace identity.[25,26,27]

In 2023, part-time workers make up almost one third of Australia's labour market, with women significantly more likely to work part-time to fit around care commitments.[28] Although working fewer hours, what little research there is suggests that part-timers are expected to produce '100% of the outputs in 60 or 80% of the hours—and for 60 or 80% of the salary'.[29]

While one might assume that the feminised care sectors would offer a more circular/collaborative management style, with men *still* dominating leadership roles, and with women who do hold senior positions often 'leading' with male-coded behaviours, it is unsurprising that the system, as experienced by many women workers, is broken.[30,31]

In one of the wealthiest countries in the world, one with a long tradition of 'sisterhood'/feminism, it seems that women themselves haven't changed as much as *the economies* in which we provision our work.[32]

Genevieve Vaughan explains the role of gender (stereotypes) in this system:

> The market and masculation of capitalism and patriarchy have developed into a dominant paradigm and a paradigm of dominance, and they have become the basic, though unacknowledged, underlying pattern or metaphor for all our thinking.[33]

Similarly, Eversberg and Smeltzer write:

> In the dominant cultural imaginary of growth societies, this figure of the growth subject is powerfully gendered: it is coded as masculine. The classical figure of the white bourgeois, the agent of capitalist expansion, is that of a man seeking to optimally deploy the resources at his disposal so as to ratio-

> nally and purposefully enlarge them ... This does not mean that only men are growth subjects and that others are not, nor that all men have incorporated growth subjectivity in the same way and to the same degree – but rather that key aspects of growth subjectivities are coded as masculine due to the historical genealogies of their cultural understandings. In fact, within modern growth societies the cultural, social and economic logics that structure people's everyday experience are so deeply impregnated with 'masculine' principles of expansion, exclusion and competition that these leave a mark on everybody, regardless of gender.[34]

So masculation doesn't solely reward men; nor, conversely, does it reward 'all men'. Between gender, race, ability, LGBTIQA+ identity, social class and other, innumerable 'intersections' of lived experience, we see how the binaries of the growth paradigm, the hierarchies stepped into the pyramid of capital, endure in a destructive dynamism that can only end as other 'pyramid' or 'Ponzi schemes' inevitably end: in carnage.

A 'Maternal' Gift Economy?

In the so-called 'maternal' gift paradigm, founder Genevieve Vaughan explicitly links a universal experience of receiving gifts of nurture, typically from mothers but in her later writings, all 'motherers'. Human beings need care and nourishment to survive beyond infanthood and this care*gifting* and gift receiving is fundamentally relational, communicated through language and shared understanding.

Maternal gift economy advocates call for a 'matriation' or 'rematriation' of the social order; an new economic paradigm based upon principles of gift-giving which, like those of the motherer/parent, are typically *other-focused*.

This model presents an alternative to the values of exchange capitalism; its ego-oriented and individualistic rationality, its power relations of dominance, differentiated value and inequality.

Degrowth advocates, decolonial feminists and the maternal gift economy movement all propose similar economic alternatives to modern capitalism, many aligning in presenting a gifting paradigm of social organisation, one based upon the more circular socio-economic formations of traditional and Indigenous cultures, regenerative and de-commodified ways of living which recognise the essential mutuality of coexistence with all living things, and which typically also include a strong focus on the stewardship and sustainability of Earth's natural resources as a key component of any proposed new cultural/economic paradigm.

In a similar way we see ecofeminists link Indigenous and pre-modern practices explicitly with *the feminine*, even positioning women as natural custodians of the environment. Sometimes regarded as 'the feminism of the South', ecofeminism draws on synergies between female reproductive biology and the life-giving properties of 'Mother Earth'. Although there has been critique of ecofeminist theory from the time of its inception in the 1990s, ecofeminists did much in linking the subordination of women and that of the natural world under patri-colonial capitalism, highlighting the ways in which this 'othering' allowed for a male appropriation of both technology and 'rational thinking'.

As a theoretical framework, ecofeminism articulates how the dualistic and patriarchal nature of capitalism not only serves to subjugate the feminine, but has also coded the natural environment with feminine (and therefore less valuable) qualities. Although ecofeminism and maternal/matriarchal gift economy models have rightly been interrogated as essentialist, their common critique of a destructive and neo-patriarchal growth capitalism, one only magnified under 'neoliberal fundamentalism', has helped expose the illusory nature of the hierarchies and value propositions of the pyramid of capital, with its *fundamentally economic* dynamism of othering.[35,36]

If Growth Is Patriarchal, Then Why Not (Re)matriation?

That 'The Economy' is in fact a social construct, and not a real or tangible thing, is an important argument against the growth paradigm. As degrowth scholarship matures, we need not only to focus on developing socio-economic alternatives and rapidly progressing transformative change, but equally, to *decolonise the growth imaginary*, permanently disrupting exchange logic to instead co-create a much more collective version of our cultures and 'imagination infrastructure', a new discourse to drive sustainable and equitable living.[37,38,39]

For some gift economy advocates, this decolonising process would be hastened by the adoption of *maternal values,* even of 'matriarchal' social structures; a 'rematriation' of modern culture which they avow can offer a genuinely paradigmatic response to modern patriarchal capitalism.

Bernadette Muthien, a teacher of modern matriarchal studies, believes the 'structuring principles' of a matriarchal economy should be:

- Concrete rather than abstract in world;
- Not mother rule but non-hierarchical;
- Consensus (unanimity), consultative, participatory, democratic;
- Distribution (sharing) as opposed to accumulation (hoarding);
- 'Meeting of needs' instead of having 'power over';
- Motherly or matriarchal men;
- Humane society;
- Radically oriented towards life (not war industry);
- Political action always spiritual in matriarchy (vs. detachment in patriarchy);
- All connected: science, politics, spirituality, all ad infinitum.

Muthien and other maternal gift economy advocates urge us to:

> [c]hart past strategic interventions, dreams, realities that are not mere alternatives to hetero-patriarchal capitalisms, but entirely reconfigure our cosmos.[40]

This discourse of a 'matriarchal' or 'maternal' gift economy undeniably responds to the entrenched and deeply paradigmatic nature of a growth capitalism in which commodification and exchange suffuses all of human and planetary life.

While degrowth and 'new economy' advocates continue to design, develop and disseminate more circular and sustainable ways of living, it is also critically important that we pay attention to activities and movements taking place at the grassroots of different societies and cultures.

However, as David Bollier and Silke Helfrich point out:

> The viability of bottom-up commons often depends upon supportive institutions, policy regimes and law. This is the new frontier for the Commons Sector: developing new bodies of law and policy to facilitate the practices of commoning on the ground. For this, the state must play a more active role in sanctioning and facilitating the functioning of the commons, much as it currently facilitates the functioning of corporations.[41]

In This Chapter …

We have looked at the intrinsically gendered nature of patriarchal capitalism and how it functions to reproduce itself within neoliberal free market conceptions of growth, individual liberty and choice. The so-called healthy competition of the market's 'invisible hand' denies the systemic and structural disadvantages built into the pyramid of capital, rendering them an invisible schema, Terry Leahy's 'ghost in the machine', reproducing inequality just as it reproduces privilege. Core to this is capitalism's ego-centred exchange logic and its destructive and parasitic dependence upon invisibilised practices of gift giving.

In the Next Chapter …

We will look at worker movements emerging across the global North which are challenging the corporate/business environments of late-stage capitalism, increasing the alienation of workers from the means of production.

Notes

1. Evason, N. (2016). Australian Culture: core concepts. SBS Australia. https://culturalatlas.sbs.com.au/australian-culture/australian-culture-core-concepts 28/12/2022. Accessed June 2021.
2. Brunetto, Y. (2012). Supervisor Relationships, Teamwork, Role Ambiguity and Discretionary Power: Nurses in Australia and the United Kingdom. International Journal of Public Administration Volume 35, 2012—Issue 8: Contemporary Challenges for Public Sector Human Resource Management. July 9, 2012. https://doi.org/10.1080/01900692.2012.655471. Accessed June 2021.
3. Brunetto, Y. et al. (2013). The impact of workplace relationships on engagement, well-being, commitment and turnover for nurses in Australia and the USA. Jan: Leading Global Nursing Research. https://doi.org/10.1111/jan.12165. Accessed June 2019.
4. Australian Translation Services. (2021). Australian Workplace Culture: Astounding Facts You Must Know. https://australiantranslationservices.com.au/australian-workplace-culture/. Accessed Jan 2023.
5. Risse, L. (2021). When work becomes a masculinity contest. Power to Persuade, July 14, 2021. https://www.powertopersuade.org.au/blog/when-work-becomes-a-masculinity-contest/14/7/2021?rq=Toxic%20&s=09. Accessed Aug 2021.

6. A 2018 study by McCrindle found four out of five schoolchildren in Australia had been targets of bullying, with one in five experiencing bullying weekly. See: https://mccrindle.com.au/article/topic/generation-z/research-reveals-shocking-new-statistics-of-australias-bullying-crisis/.
7. Risse. L. (2021). Ibid.
8. Vaughan, G. (2004). Ibid.
9. Risse. L. (2021). Ibid.
10. Vaughan, G. (2004). ibid.
11. Vaughan, G. (2004). Ibid.
12. Chodorow, N. (2018). Family structure and feminine personality. In *Feminism and philosophy* (pp. 199–216). Routledge. p. 2.
13. Chodorow, N. (2018). Family structure and feminine personality. In *Feminism and philosophy* (pp. 199–216). Routledge. p. 8.
14. Lynch, K. (2014). New Managerialism: The Impact on Education. Concept, Vol. 5 No. 3 Winter 2014, pp. 1–11. https://core.ac.uk/download/pdf/162673921.pdf. p. 1. Accessed June 2021.
15. Lafferty, G., & Fleming, J. (2000). The restructuring of academic work in Australia: Power, management and gender. British journal of sociology of education, 21(2), 257–267. Accessed Feb 2023.
16. McGrath, C., Roxa, T., and Bolander-Laksov, B. (2018). Change in a culture of collegiality and consensus-seeking: a double-edged sword. Higher Education Research & Development Volume 38, 2019—Issue 5. Pages 1001–1014 | Apr 15, 2019. https://doi.org/10.1080/07294360.2019.1603203.
17. Pannowitz, H., Glass, N., & Davis, K. (2009). Resisting gender-bias: Insights from Western Australian middle-level women nurses. Contemporary Nurse, 33(2), 103–119.
18. Zheng, W., Yang, B. and McLean, G.N., (2010). Linking organizational culture, structure, strategy, and organizational effectiveness: Mediating role of knowledge management. Journal of Business research, 63(7), pp. 763–771.
19. Mosadeghrad, A.M., (2014). Factors influencing healthcare service quality. International journal of health policy and management, 3(2), p. 77.
20. McGrath, C., Roxa, T., and Bolander-Laksov, B. (2018). Ibid.
21. Colnar. S et al. (2020). Quality of Healthcare Services in Focus: The Role of Knowledge Transfer, Hierarchical Organizational Structure and Trust. Knowledge Management Research & Practice. May 14, 2021. https://doi.org/10.1080/14778238.2021.1932623.
22. Aiken, L.H., Clarke, S.P., Sloane, D.M., Sochalski, J. and Silber, J.H., (2002). Hospital nurse staffing and patient mortality, nurse burnout, and job dissatisfaction. JAMA, 288(16), pp. 1987–1993.
23. Chester, L. (2012). The Australian variant of neoliberal capitalism. Neoliberalism: Beyond the free market, pp. 153–179. Pp: 162–163.

24. Nelson, A. (2022). Beyond Money. Apple Books. p. 52.
25. Pennington, A. and Stanford, J. (2020). Deunionisation and wage stagnation: A commentary on recent Reserve Bank Research. Australian Journal of Labour Law, 32(3), pp. 318–337.
26. Hamilton, R. and Nichol, M. (2021). Minimum wage regulation in Australia in the wake of the pandemic: the future of the five wage concepts? Labour & Industry: a journal of the social and economic relations of work, 31(4), pp. 405–417.
27. Brunetto, Y. et al. (2013). The impact of workplace relationships on engagement, well-being, commitment and turnover for nurses in Australia. https://doi.org/10.1111/jan.12165. Accessed June 2019.
28. Australian Bureau of Statistics. (2023). Headline estimates of employment, unemployment, underemployment, participation and hours worked from the monthly Labour Force Survey.
29. Gascoigne, C., & Kelliher, C. (2018). The transition to part-time: How professionals negotiate 'reduced time and workload' i-deals and craft their jobs. Human Relations, 71(1), 103–125. https://doi.org/10.1177/0018726717722394.
30. See Tranum, S. (2022). Supporting feminine leadership can help create a just and kinder future. The Conversation. https://theconversation.com/supporting-feminine-leadership-can-help-create-a-just-and-kinder-future-193607. Also Martinot, C. (2023) Feminine Leadership Explained: The 'Masculine' and 'Feminine' Sides of Leadership. https://management30.com/blog/feminine-leadership/. Accessed April 2023.
31. Naccarella Lucio, Osborne Richard H., Brooks Peter M. (2016) Training a system-literate care coordination workforce. Australian Health Review 40, 210–212. https://doi.org/10.1071/AH15014.
32. Kenny, K. (2022). Staging a Revolution: When Betty Rocked the Pram. Upswell Publishing.
33. Vaughan, G. (2004). Ibid.
34. Eversberg, D. and Schmelzer, M. (2023). Degrowth and Masculinities: Towards a gendered understanding of degrowth subjectivities. Degrowth Journal, May 3, 2023. https://www.degrowthjournal.org/publications/2023-05-03-degrowth-and-masculinities-towards-a-gendered-understanding-of-degrowth-subjectivities/. Accessed May 2023.
35. Mellor, M. (1992). Eco-feminism and eco-socialism: Dilemmas of essentialism and materialism. Capitalism Nature Socialism, 3(2), pp. 43–62.
36. Salleh, A., (2010). How the Ecological Footprint Is Sex-Gendered: Implications of Eco-feminism for an Eco-socialist Theory and Praxis. Eco-socialism as Politics: Rebuilding the Basis of Our Modern Civilisation, pp. 141–147.

37. Mellor, M. (1997). Women, nature and the social construction of 'economic man', Ecological Economics, Volume 20, Issue 2, 1997, Pages 129–140, ISSN 0921-8009, https://doi.org/10.1016/S0921-8009(95)00100-X.
38. Asara, V., Profumi, E. and Kallis, G., (2013). Degrowth, democracy and autonomy. *Environmental Values*, *22* (2), pp. 217–239.
39. Liegey, V., and Nelson, A. (2020). Exploring Degrowth. Pluto Press.
40. Muthien, B. (2011). Rematriation of Women-Centred (feminist) Indigenous Knowledge. Audio transcript: http://gift-economy.com/rematriation-of-women-centered-feminist-indigenous-knowledge/. Accessed Oct 2021.
41. Bollier, D., and Helfrich, S. (Eds) (2012). Introduction to the Wealth of the Commons, the Commons as a Transformative Vision. Commons Strategy Group. P. Introduction.

CHAPTER 9

Pathways Out of Capitalism

Abstract Further interrogating the role of gender in growth capitalism, this chapter broadens out to explore cultural norms of individualism and how these have overtaken a more collectivist formation of humanity's imagination infrastructure, our cultural and social values. This chapter suggests that, only by disrupting entrenched dualisms which underpin our destructive growth paradigm, can we conquer the cult of self and begin the shift towards a more inclusive and collectivist degrowth model. Theorising that the aggressive workplace behaviours of women are socially constructed and 'masculated', the author also explores the 'radical selfishness' of some men in the context of the coronavirus pandemic, and how this worked to their detriment, with significantly higher disease burden and death rates from COVID seen in men the world over. Looking beyond sociological understanding of gendered behaviours, the author then presents 'hard science' relevant in the context of the pandemic, to argue that a '(re)matriation' of human culture is a necessary response to the still hyper-masculine machinations of an exchange capitalism that is destroying our planet.

Keywords Capitalism • Masculinity • Selfishness • Imagination infrastructure • Culture • Plasticity • Neoliberalism • Maternal • Matriarchal • Rematriation • Gender • Masculate • Patriarchy

M. Jordan, *Women's Work in the Pandemic Economy*,
https://doi.org/10.1007/978-3-031-40154-1_9

Introduction

What pandemics, climate change and other evidence of 'systems' disruption tells us, as Martin Luther King Jr. observed in 1963, is that 'all life is interrelated, all men [sic] are caught in an inescapable network of mutuality ... Whatever affects one directly, affects all indirectly.[1]

The COVID crisis, as the two disparate examples of women working presented here show, is both an *outcome* of the systemic destructions of capitalism and *a driver*. What can we learn from them then, about the role of gender in helping us to identify and establish potential pathways out of capitalism?

Masculinity as Radical Selfishness

Theorising that the aggressive and selfish behaviours of women on the pandemic frontline were masculated, or male-coded, is not to suggest that women are intrinsically kinder/nicer - *better* than men. Nor that women's 'misbehaviour' in the workplace is not a problem for feminism, where discussion of it seems at best scant. Rather, my aim here is to underscore the role that economic systems play in shaping and gendering human behaviour.

As theorised in previous chapters, male-coded behaviours are essential to the growth paradigm and are therefore systemitised to reward workers, whatever their gender. We see this manifest in neoliberal precepts of competition, individualism and hierarchy structured into the modern labour market, but also in the ways that these principles still reflect and reproduce value propositions dating back to colonisation, as colonisation itself endures.

In the context of systematised and gendered economic behaviours, it is perhaps less important to focus only on 'male' and 'female' workers therefore, or on differentiated work conditions in female- and/or male-dominated industries, than it is to look at the *macroeconomic settings* of labour, and the potential role of disrupting gender (and other) binaries in challenging the status quo, as some degrowth thinkers now suggest.[2]

As noted earlier, the coronavirus pandemic wrought highly gendered outcomes: a 'pink recession' for women and higher rates of death and serious illness for men. Both of these were social determined outcomes, neither had a 'natural', nor a biological causation.

Gender also played a further role in the pandemic according to feminist commentator Rebecca Solnit, one articulated in the 'radical selfishness' of (some) men's behaviour. The egocentrism exteriorised in men often refusing to wear facemasks, or to follow other, usually government mandated, virus precautions. Again, this is not an outcome of any biological essentialism, but rather a 'natural' extension of the rights' discourse of neoliberal individualism. [3] This is both because behaviours deemed to be 'selfcare' are of course female-coded, and yet paradoxically, caring *beyond self*, for the collective good, is *also* female-coded behaviour.

Writing in 2020, Solnit tells us:

> Wearing masks, it turns out, is not manly, when the definition of manly is not having to do fuck-all out of concern for others. There are a lot of other things that turn out not to be manly, including caring about climate change and environmental problems, and even, according to some studies recycling (and others, handwashing). Taking care of things is not manly … a definition of masculinity as radical selfishness, [that has] taken a huge toll in American lives … [it] peaks at an intersection between whiteness and maleness, with plenty of white women on board.[4]

We can better understand these masculinities as socially constructed by examining the very different ways that cultures define 'manhood' and what a 'real man' looks like; and that, as anthropologist David Gilmore reminds us, '*boys have to be encouraged, sometimes actually forced, by social sanctions to undertake efforts toward a culturally defined manhood, which by themselves they might not do.*'[5]

Beyond these sociological insights into gendered behaviour, there is also 'hard science' which is relevant in the context of the pandemic. A 2017 study exploring gendered differences in social choices found male neural reward systems to be 'more stimulated by self-centredness', while women's are stimulated *when* and *by helping others.* I.e., females are 'more sensitive to prosocial rewards', but for reasons that are socially constructed.[6]

Other research also positions men as more 'self-absorbed'. A 30-year, longitudinal US study for example, involving 475,000 participants, found men consistently scored higher in tests for narcissism than women, and at all ages.[7] That this (male) gendered self-interest has both a macro- and a micro-economic dimension is undeniable. It bolsters the powers of the capital class by driving down collective (worker) action, and it also resonates in the institution of home/family, where we see that even those men in dual-income households still hoard the power, securing significantly more leisure time than their female 'partners'.[8]

So gendered difference has both a sociological and a biological dimension, with the brain learning to reward ego-oriented and individualistic behaviours in men, both through repetition, and via the positive social responses that these behaviours attract. In a similar way, the other-focused caregiving and nurturing behaviours more typical of to women 'may be the result of education and/or cultural expectations … through the internalization of cultural norms.' [9]

Thus patriarchal capitalism works to shape our economic behaviours in its own image.

It is here in this narrative that is again useful to consider the concept of a *re-matriation* of society; the extent to which an ascendancy of female-coded values might better function to meet the challenges and inadequacies of growth capitalism than our current, neo-patriarchal cultural settings.

Barbara Alice Mann speaks of a 'rematriation of the truth'. In a similar call to pre-capitalist social organisation, Colombian academic Andrea Dolmetsch also describes how a 'matriarchal' discourse has the substance needed to challenge parti-colonial capitalism in a deep and paradigmatic way:[10]

> Rematriation … refers to reclaiming ancestral remains. Amongst many other things, spirituality, culture, knowledge, resources … back to Mother Earth and return to origins, to life and co-creation rather [than the] patriarchal destruction of colonisation … can be very powerful, totally relevant to both our thinking and our activism.[11]

For Dolmetsch:

> We need to chart past strategic interventions, dreams, realities that are not mere alternatives to hetero-patriarchal capitalisms, but entirely reconfigure our cosmos…rematriation can contribute to concrete transformation of heteropatriarchy. Our idea is always to not just think about, **to act on.**[12]

This concept of matriation has some alignment with both eco and decolonial feminisms, linking the (divine) feminine with the life-giving and nurturing properties of the 'Mother' (Earth). As such, it works outside of/beyond questions of historical veracity relating to the actual existence of premodern matriarchal societies, to instead shine light on their inverse: the hyper-masculine nature of modern capitalism.

For academic and activist Vandana Shiva:

> The rule of money and men, which is what patriarchy basically is, misunderstands the world. It misunderstands reality, misunderstands humanity… I

> see it misunderstanding creativity in its most basic level. It is the lie that the constructs of men and money are the creative force of the universe. Capital is a construct, but it becomes the creative force in extracting from the gifts of nature, and the gifts of humanity, and of society…and [in] the denial of nature's creativity, of women's creativity, of the creativity of indigenous cultures, [Indigenous] economies … [It] is the violence we witness on a daily basis and a lot of people think that that violence of colonialisation is over, but I see it intensifying.[13]

With gender identity strongly linked to socially constructed behaviours, it wasn't surprising to identify the a highly gendered order in the gift economies of the three Good Karma Networks, where both the activities/labours taking place, and also what might be framed as the 'workplace culture', aligned palpably with gift economy and degrowth principles.

Membership across all 35+ GKNs was/is predominantly female, as noted earlier. Yet *The Gift Highway* data also identified a good number of men actively participating in gift-giving, requesting and receiving practices. Of the 272 posts which fell into the 'COVID-specific' category for example, 33.9% of total keyword posts, although 89.3% were attributable to women, a not insignificant 10.7% were made by men.

A similar gender breakdown was seen in the post categories of 'material' and 'non-material' gifting.[14] Although women were responsible for 93.4% of posts offering 'material gifts' such as unwanted or used goods, and for 92.7% of posts offering 'non-material gifts': advice, humorous tales and so forth, the remainder were from men (a very few from 'gender unknown'). These distinct patterns in gender engagement only slightly shifted in *requests* for material and non-material gifts, where women comprised 87.5% and 86.4% of total 'request' posts respectively, and men/unknown genders making up the remaining 10% and 15% of gift requests.

Interestingly, the gender bias identified was less marked in one of the Networks studied, GKN 'C'. An explanation for this may lie with the fact that the municipality this GKN covered has a higher male demographic than the other areas analysed; and also a younger overall population profile. Although the GKNs are not of course wholly representative of their local demographic, Network 'B' has a significant Chinese-speaking population for example, the increased male activity in Network 'C' is an interesting anomaly. It supports the argument that there is nothing biologically inherent in practices of gifting, or in a gift economy model, despite the appeal of the 'maternal' discourse. It perhaps also signals that younger men are less masculated than their fathers and grandfathers.

Interestingly, over half of the male posts in GKN ‘A’ (54.3%), fell into the category of ‘*non-material gift requests*’. Also interestingly, these chiefly comprised requests for information, and not personal guidance or advice.

The gender breakdown across the three networks can be seen in the charts below (see Figs. 9.1, 9.2 and 9.3).[15]

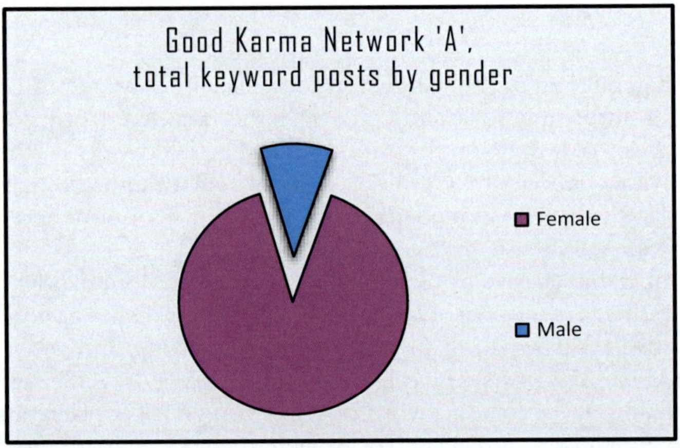

Fig. 9.1 Good Karma Network ‘A’, total keyword posts by gender identity 2020–2021

Fig. 9.2 Good Karma Network ‘B’, total keyword posts by gender identity, 2020–2021

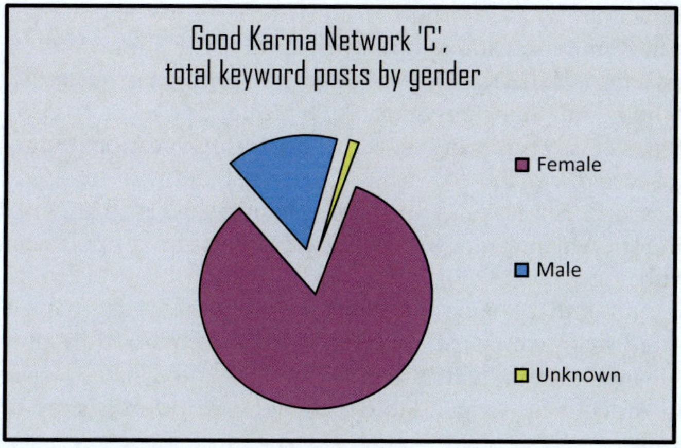

Fig. 9.3 Good Karma Network 'C', total keyword posts by gender identity, 2020–2021

The Care-full Workplace

If we think of the Good Karma Networks as a sort of voluntary equivalent of the 'businesses of care', we again see a highly feminised workforce—but one behaving in very different and less toxic ways to those described by women administering a commodified care. The 'gift economy workplace' also demonstrates that it is a culture where men are not only free, but *encouraged to engage* in the female-coded behaviours that patriarchal norms typically discourage. That GKN C, with its younger and more masculine demographic, had greater male engagement may indicate that the foundations of gender, including the gendered nature of caregifting, are already being disrupted.

From here, we can understand that the bullying behaviours of women workers during and preceding COVID, are not inherent to female biology, to gender stereotypes and 'mean girls' tropes. What instead becomes apparent, are the ways in which (gendered) behaviours are undeniably linked to the *economic paradigm* within which they are situated.

Thus, neoliberal exchange capitalism will always prioritise growth—*profit*—never fully or equitably rewarding workers and women workers even less, as much feminised labour must remain devalued and invisibilised for growth to 'succeed'. Ever-mounting pressures upon workers, whether women, men or another gender identity, to continue to feed into the capital pyramid whatever the costs, can be seen in the emergence of new social movements expressing worker dissatisfaction and frustration. Dissatisfaction is particularly notable in Australia's businesses of care, where the mainly female workforce, typically powerless to deliver care in the *relational way* that workers with a nurturing vocation might intuitively prefer, a care*gifting* linked with the maternal and with 'motherers' of any gender, are either leaving nursing, teaching and so forth in droves, or stuck in jobs which can have a highly negative impact upon women workers' wellbeing.

The outcome of such growth-focused settings is that the female-dominated work sectors of the 21st century are marred by both burnout and bullying; with individual female workers—like male workers in other sectors—effectively 'expendable', even as workforce gaps and shortages swell.

As Michael Flood writes:

> Our world is a deeply unequal one. Systemic inequalities which disadvantage women and advantage men are visible around the globe. Whether one looks at political power and authority, economic resources and decision-making, sexual and family relations, or media and culture, one finds gender inequalities. These are sustained in part by constructions of masculinity—by the cultural meanings associated with being a man, the practices which men adopt, and the collective and institutional organisation of men's lives and relations.[16]

'Imagination Infrastructure' and the Plastic Brain

That human behaviour is immutable is a common conception. After all, many hundreds of years of religious and scientific discourse tell us so. Acting outside of entrenched and largely universal gender roles still typically invites punishment, just as acting *within* these cultural constraints mostly rewards us. There is undoubtedly a wholesale cognitive dissonance in this, as conforming to one of only two rigidly defined and normative gender identities is not only difficult, but often dangerous to both men and women. It is no wonder therefore, that gender becomes an increasingly contested subjectivity under late-stage capitalism and from here, a priority for degrowth philosophies. So how do we start to transform such deeply-rooted ways of living and relating to the world?[17]

In the UK, in the wake of the pandemic, we see new money being directed towards decision-making processes described as 'community-led collective imagination'; to 'the growing community of people designing and practicing collective imagination' in response to the polycrises humanity now faces. This funding appears to recognise the urgent need to build social infrastructure which supports grassroots democratic participation and recognises its potential as a long-term response to social fragmentation.

While admitting, 'how this infrastructuring is defined and resourced is an ongoing inquiry', and its 'need to be invested in over the long term', this concept of 'imagination infrastructure'—really of a collective social culture—is useful in the context of the two studies presented, in that it recognises that our brains/imaginations/cultures are actually 'plastic' in nature, mutable in ways that some see as more feminine or circular in nature, as opposed to the fixed/rigid rationality inherent to patriarchal masculinities.

The UK initiative is interesting because it speaks to emerging 'methodologies and practices of collective imagination', which have the potential to shift us beyond individualistic and supposedly 'consumer-centred' economic settings and practices, where we typically see ego-oriented decision-making dominate collectivist thinking.

To encourage and embolden gift giving and related degrowth/gifting economic practices therefore, perhaps we don't need only to rely on intellectual arguments against growth capitalism, but might instead progress real change through the creation and incentivising of this new social infrastructure; of decision-making; environments which stipulate horizontalism and are therefore also better designed to platform voices at the margins.[18]

Olivia Oldham describes these new imaginaries, as 'the mythologies and infrastructures around which we construct our societies'. For Oldham, current cultural settings 'stop us from imagining, and from there creating, "future trajectories"'—as the climate emergency shows.[19] In a similar vein, Laura Bear identifies the malignant grip that 'sociotechnical imaginaries have on our collective imagination', including how these govern 'ways of structuring and relating to capital and labour'.[20]

In *Generation Expendable?*, we saw the imagination infrastructure of a growth mentality permeate the pandemic workplace, resulting in workers from the 'nurturing' professions engaging in bullying, intimidation, victimisation and other harmful workplace behaviours which are rewarded and reproduced by a market hegemony promoting and incentivising selfishness as 'rational' human behaviour.

This conception of being able to purposefully create infrastructure of the collective human imagination fundamentally challenges the rigidity of rational economic man, yet fascinatingly, its elemental fluidity may actually align with the 'science' of behavioural economics. In the 'algorithmic culture' of our increasingly 'smart' twenty-first century 'internet of things', even a 10 second pause over a 'sponsored' social media post can be monetised; as we see increasingly see in what Hall bluntly describes as 'the commodification of everything'.[21,22]

We may currently make choices which reinforce our (gendered) identities, but we are just as able to encourage economic behaviours of *gifting;* if only we practice them frequently enough for it to start to recraft our collective imagination, or cultural infrastructure, or economic heuristics—whatever we want to call it. When we consider the science of brain plasticity, promote new models of collective thinking, it is possible to at last see we have the power to encourage behaviours which will shape social/cultural/economic environments—including new and degrowth ways of living—in good ways, ways which broach traditional social binaries and inequalities.

Genevieve Vaughan identifies heteronormativity as another biformity underpinning and maintaining capitalism:

> Those who are themselves neither the one, nor one-of-the-many related to the one as modeled in the patriarchal family, are also…irrelevant. Anyone who does not accept the norm of heterosexuality can be seen as dangerous and socially deviant… Of course many homosexuals and transgendered people performatively repeat the power relations they find in the society around them (Butler 1990) but being beyond the norm of normativity brings with it a revolutionary potential which could be empowered if the connections between heterosexism and the economy of the market were made more explicit. Unfortunately the market and heterosexism validate each other in many different ways…a hall of mirrors without seeing the connections … that is perhaps why homosexuality and transgender seem so threatening to the economic right wing.[23]

While we look to new social imaginaries, particularly to the decolonising of the growth imaginary, challenging not only gender *roles*, but the *gender dichotomy itself*, will prove fundamental in unfolding the pivot from growth capitalism towards a survivable future. While some of this disassembling of binaries is highlighted in degrowth theory we more commonly see it emergent in a nascent 'gender warrior generation'; one which mixes gender identities and pronouns faster, and, I would argue, in a more subversive way, than ever before. Decades of feminist (and queer) activism has undoubtedly emancipated women from the home; but ironically, at least in the context of Australia's women workers—it has perhaps only transposed their essential function to the capital pyramid, shifting 'god's police' from behind the twitching curtain and into the masculated corridors of corporate feminism.

Feminist activism remains important and ever urgent, yet must also work to understand and expose the current limitations of its own imagination infrastructure; inviting in processes of deep decolonisation and interrogation of a dualism of gender, activities which have the potential to disrupt and reimagine outdated and liberal ontologies and processes of decision-making, returning to the grassroots to include and embrace *all* the voices of 'other':

> We are living in a distinctive moment when neoliberal capitalism and neopatriarchy converge. Male dominance is no mere footnote to this new historic settlement. It is central. And feminism is decisive in the resistance.[24]

In This Chapter …

We have stepped back from the ethnographic research to further interrogate the critical role of gender and related binaries to the growth paradigm; the ways in which cultural norms function to underpin individualist notions of identity over a more collectivist formation of imagination infrastructure. While some see newly diverse gender and sexual identities as threatening (to 'women'), this chapter shows that they are in fact pivotal to disrupting the entrenched (gender) norms and binaries which underpin capitalism. Only by embracing fluidity can we challenge rigidity. Similarly, only by creating an imagination infrastructure which platforms the voice of the other, can we overshadow and even conquer the cult of self and begin the shift towards a more inclusive and polycentric degrowth.

In the Next Chapter …

I detail some of the worker movements seeking to challenge neoliberal fundamentalism. Following decades of deunionisation however, these mostly fragmented activities of resistance offer little hope for the deep and systemic change so urgently needed.

Notes

1. King, M. L. (1963). Speech transcript at: https://kinginstitute.stanford.edu/sites/mlk/files/letterfrombirmingham_wwcw.pdf. Accessed Dec 2023.
2. Abazeri, M. (2022). Decolonial Feminisms and Degrowth. Futures Volume 136, February 2022, 102902.
3. Solnit, R. (2020). Masculinity As Radical Selfishness: the maskless men of the pandemic. Literary Hub, May 29, 2020. https://lithub.com/masculinity-as-radical-selfishness-rebecca-solnit-on-the-maskless-men-of-the-pandemic/. Accessed June 2020.
4. Solnit, R. (2020). Ibid.
5. Gilmore, D. (1991). Manhood in the Making: Cultural Concepts of Masculinity. Cited in Plummer, D. Masculinity and terror: the missing conversation. The Conversation, Oct 9, 2014. https://theconversation.com/masculinity-and-terror-the-missing-conversation-32276. Accessed June 2019.
6. Soutschek, A., Burke, C.J., Raja Beharelle, A. *et al.* (2017). The dopaminergic reward system underpins gender differences in social preferences. *Nat Hum Behav* **1**, 819–827 (2017). https://doi.org/10.1038/s41562-017-0226-y.
7. Grijalva, E., Newman, D., Tay, L., Donnellan, M. B., Harms, P. D., Robins, R.W., & Yan. (2015). Gender differences in narcissism: A meta-analytic review. *Psychological Bulletin*, Vol 141(2), Mar 2015, 261-310. https://doi.org/10.1037/a0038231.
8. Feng, Z., Zou, K., & Savani, K. (2023). Cultural antecedents of virus transmission: Individualism is associated with lower compliance with social distancing rules during the COVID-19 pandemic. *Journal of Personality and Social Psychology*, Vol 124(3), Mar 2023, 461–482. https://doi.org/10.1037/pspa0000322. Accessed April 2023.
9. Jacobs, T. (2017). New Evidence That Women Are Less Selfish Than Men. *Specific Standard*. https://psmag.com/news/new-evidence-women-are-less-selfish-than-men. Accessed June 2019.
10. Mann, B.A. (2011). Rematriation of the truth. Audio transcript from Women's Worlds conference, Ottawa. July 7, 2011.
11. Muthien, B. (2011). Rematriating Western Ways of Thinking. Women's Worlds, Ottawa, July 2011. Audio transcript: http://gift-economy.com/many-voices/.
12. Dolmetsch, A. (2011). Rematriating Western Ways of Thinking Panel at Women's Worlds, Ottawa, July 2011.
13. Shiva, V. (2022). Virtual Salon #25 Misuse and Abuse of Language. Maternal Gift Economy, https://www.maternalgifteconomymovement.org/salon-25-misuse-and-abuse-of-language/. Accessed June 2022.

14. A single post might sometimes fit into both categories of material and non-material gifting, if for example, it included an offer of both a physical good/item and a non-material gift such as sharing thoughtful advice or good tidings to the community.
15. Jordan, M. (2023). Unpublished data from The Gift Highway, Grassroots Research Studio, 2021–2023. Available from info@grassrootsresearch.com.au.
16. Flood, M. (2015). Men and gender equality. In M. G. Flood & R. Howson (Eds.), Engaging Men in Building Gender Equality (pp. 1–31). Newcastle upon Tyne: Cambridge Scholars Publishing.
17. Flood, M. (2018). Australian study reveals the dangers of 'toxic masculinity' to men and those around them. The Conversation. Oct 16, 2018. https://theconversation.com/australian-study-reveals-the-dangers-of-toxic-masculinity-to-men-and-those-around-them-104694. Accessed Nov 2022.
18. Baumann, K., Stokes, B., Bar, F., & Caldwell, B. (2017). Infrastructures of the imagination: Community design for speculative urban technologies. In *Proceedings of the 8th International Conference on Communities and Technologies* (pp. 266–269).
19. Oldham, O. (2021). Imagination Infrastructure — What Do We Mean? *Medium*, May 1, 2021. https://oliviaoldham.medium.com/imagination-infrastructure-abd96262fff6 Accessed April 2023.
20. Bear, L. (2020). Speculation: a political economy of technologies of imagination. Economy and Society, pp. 1–15. Published online: 18 Feb 2020. https://doi.org/10.1080/03085147.2020.1715604.
21. Rose, K., Eldridge, S., & Chapin, L. (2015). The internet of things: An overview. The internet society (ISOC), 80, 1–50.
22. Hall, D. (2022). 'Commodification of everything' arguments in the social sciences: Variants, specification, evaluation, critique. Environment and Planning A: Economy and Space, 0308518X221128305.
23. Vaughan, G. (2004). Heterosexual Economics: Gift-giving and Exchange. A Radically Different World View Is Possible. The Gift Economy Inside and Outside of Patriarchal Capitalism. November 12–14, 2004.
24. Campbell, B. (2014). Neoliberal neopatriarchy: the case for gender revolution. Open Democracy, Jan 6, 2104. https://www.opendemocracy.net/en/5050/neoliberal-neopatriarchy-case-for-gender-revolution/. Accessed April 2023.

CHAPTER 10

Antiwork

Abstract The *Generation Expendable?* study had uncovered much evidence of worker burnout, with the so-called 'Great Resignation' that occurred during the pandemic seen partly as a response to deteriorating work conditions. Within the context of an increasingly precarious and fragmented labour market, deunionisation means that the privilege of 'antiwork'—organising for better workplace conditions, exploring new work opportunities or even being able to opt for early retirement, are privileges only some can access. Without the strength of collective action, the new worker 'movements' that have emerged to articulate worker dissatisfaction with the disease of labour under late-stage capitalism are typically individualised, with COVID only exacerbating and highlighting poor work conditions.

Keywords Antiwork • Capitalism • Anticapitalism • Neoliberalism • Fragmentation • Deunionisation • Burnout • Corporate feminism • Girlboss • Casualisation • Degrowth

Introduction

The fragmentation of workers' rights is a defining principle of neoliberal economics. In Australia, as in other countries, it has driven a sharp decline in unionisation and other forms of collective worker 'bargaining'. In

M. Jordan, *Women's Work in the Pandemic Economy*,
https://doi.org/10.1007/978-3-031-40154-1_10

male-dominated sectors such as manufacturing, once-proud national industries have dwindled away in an increasingly competitive global market[1]

In the female-dominated care industries, even with above average union membership of teachers and nurses, the shift from a predominantly state-led service model to a 'free market', competition with multinational corporations able to prioritise 'efficiency' through economies of scale, has arguably led to a 'race to the bottom' in terms of staffing ratios and workloads. 'Efficiencies' which resonate across the labour market.[2,3,4,5,6]

The coronavirus pandemic has exposed the very real dangers of workforce casualisation across the world. In Australia, casual labour accounted for around two-thirds of Australia's job losses by mid-2020. [7,8] The number of casual employees fell from 2.6 million in March of 2020, to 2.1 million by May, although it eventually recovered to 2.5 million by November 2020.[9] Like other countries, these jobs losses, with potential long-term financial implications, fell hardest upon women with caring responsibilities.

While technology enabled millions to 'bring the office home', improving work/life balance for some, for others, the blurring of place of work and designated work hours meant they were effectively 'sleeping at the office'.[10,11,12]

Naarm's succession of economic lockdowns eventually wound down after a total of 262 days in mid-October 2021, with the introduction of QR code monitoring and vaccination programs.[13] As the economy opened up, workers were at first encouraged, and later pressured to return to the workplace, particularly office workers based in the Naarm's now ghostly 'CBD' (central business district), where shops, coffee bars and other small businesses heavily rely on their custom.

It took some time in fact, before workers made a strong return to the workplace, with the new 'hybrid' working model presenting some succour to the drudgery of the daily commute and ever-pressured work cultures. But not for all.[14,15] While not the 'great resignation', or 'great retirement' claimed in the US, the pandemic nevertheless jump-started a change in working patterns for Australians also. Here, instead of simply changing jobs or taking early retirement however, a trend of workers selling up metropolitan homes to take up a 'sea-change/tree-change' remote working lifestyle, became the new demographic.[16,17,18]

For workers not able to afford retirement, or to negotiate working from home, such as women workers in essential service industries typically located in the major cities, the return to normal patterns of worker life must have brought mixed feelings.

In other parts of the world, the pandemic had seen workers newly cognisant of work/life *imbalance*. A malaise of worker dissatisfaction that had emerged prior to COVID was now notable in Australia too, particularly so in sectors which had borne the brunt of the pandemic frontline, with many seeing a very real decline in work conditions.[19,20,21] Writing in 2023, Australia is seeing a mass of teachers and teaching aides, nurses, aged care workers and other paid caregivers, exiting the businesses of care capitalism.[22]

While the long term economic and health effects of the coronavirus crisis are yet to be fully seen, what is undeniable is the still-open wound upon the labour market and on workers.

Rage Rooms, 'Screamatoria' and Dropping the Hot Potato

Worker dissatisfaction, disengagement, and burnout has swiftly developed in the workplaces of the global North across the last 10–15 years, as the cost of living has sharply risen, and workers' rights and wages have flatlined. A 2019 survey by US jobsite Monster.com shows, for example, that around 85% of US workers admit to having 'cried at work'; 52% to having lost their temper.[23] It is a zeitgeist of worker discontent indisputably linked to neoliberal work practices. Unless we see radical change, it will likely only sharpen.[24,25,26]

Without the collectivist 'muscle' of the 20th century union movement, today's working classes are forced into *individualised* tactics to push against our modern '*hustle culture*'; its 'intense focus on productivity, ambition, and success, with little regard for rest, self-care, or any sense of work-life balance.'[27,28]

Replacing strike action, we now see the emergence of 'antiwork movements'. Although these had materialised before COVID, antiwork activities have grown exponentially since 2020. In September 2022, US 'business bible' Fortune Magazine described the antiwork movement as characterised by practices such as 'quiet quitting', whereby workers refuse tasks and responsibilities outside of the work stipulated in their contracts.

A similar, minimalist approach has appeared in Japan and in China, where the practice of *tangping* or 'lying flat' has become not so much a strategy, as a symbolic statement of employee recognition of the importance of a decent life *outside of work*.[29,30,31]

In an increasingly precarious labour market, where wages often lag far behind essential costs such as housing affordability, costs of living, and where workplace conditions and cultures are often highly stressed, it is of little surprise that the over-developed countries of the global North are marked by a zeitgeist of worker disillusion and burnout. That COVID has further encouraged and exposed pitiable work conditions is irrefutable. Yet with fragmented employment configurations/'business as usual' in the twenty-first century, workers can only respond and resist in fragmented ways, not collectively.

In July of 2022, Forbes magazine wrote:

> Work is becoming increasingly more complex as organizations decide the best way to continue after the initial shock of the pandemic ... Employees find themselves inundated with requests and tasks coming at them from multiple directions, whether that's phone calls, Slack messages, Zoom Meetings, or casual conversations in the break room. In many ways, the modern workflow has become a game of hot potato... expecting others to grab them and hand them off to the next person, but more often than not, this work gets lost.[32]

While working from home during COVID was a blessing for some workers, Forbes notes that in the US, 'the toll of isolation on employee wellbeing', and a blurring of worker responsibilities even in well-defined occupations, means that *'employees are assigned tasks, often without context'*, driving the *'combination of being overwhelmed and overworked ... lead[ing] to feelings of anxiety and burnout'*.[33]

In the neoliberal market economies of the global North, some new forms of resistance have an almost *primal* element.[34] In the UK, we see a phenomena of 'screamatoria': businesses which offer (workers) '*enclosed and private spaces where* [you] *can go to scream your heart out*'.[35] In a similar vein, we see 'Rage Rooms' for workers, places where they can pay to vent their disenchantment in 'safe' ways, such as by smashing ceramics. Although such businesses were originally designed as 'fun' or leisure activities, as one proprietor explained to The Guardian in 2022:

> It's not just 'fun' anymore: people have a real reason to come in.[36]

At this particular establishment, staff had noted their clientele comprising, *'a lot of people who work in hospitality – and primary school teachers'*.[37]

R/ANTIWORK

While the 'antiwork' discourse may have its roots in anarchist and socialist economic critique, it has broadened in reach in recent years, to become an almost mainstream response to exponential productivity pressures upon employees. Yet, while the antiwork movement may articulate widespread discontent with the hegemony of late-stage capitalism, just like neoliberalism, it is individualised, fragmented and even commodified, as rage rooms, screamatoria and a booming 'wellbeing' industry all demonstrate.

Where once we had industrial action such as strikes, we now more typically see worker resistance brought into a loose collective on *social media* threads. For example, the r/antiwork 'sub thread' on web forum Reddit not only attracts members/users championing a work-free life, but also workers advocating for offices and factories 'free from toxic working conditions and cultures, wage slavery, and the poor treatment of employees.'[38,39]

The impact of the pandemic in driving this antiwork culture can actually be tracked on Reddit statistics which show that the sub thread had only a small following in 2020, but with the *'mass lay-offs and a huge shift in working conditions'* that COVID wrought, the r/antiwork 'subreddit channel' exploded in popularity and at the close of 2021, *'had grown from 100,000 to one million subscribers. Today it has over two million subscribers.'*[40]

A once 'performative workaholism' has retreated in the context of the pandemic, with workers newly appreciating that a '*social contract that normalizes systemic exploitation and repression in the name of capitalist* growth' isn't perhaps worth signing up for. Indeed, 'baffled about what the social contract entails under the neoliberal regime, the dwindling middle class, most of which is in fact the embattled working class is becoming increasingly poorer.'[41,42]

The 'r/antiwork' subreddit has global engagement but, fascinatingly, Oceania/Australia makes up the third largest cohort of followers.[43] On a tech platform known for its predominantly male membership, that the r/antiwork subthread also shows unusually high engagement with female workers is but further evidence of worker malaise resulting from unsatisfactory conditions of and at work.[44,45]

Burnout

As noted earlier, *Generation Expendable?* had uncovered much evidence of worker burnout, a condition recognised by the World Health Organisation (WHO), as '*chronic workplace stress that has not been successfully managed … including feelings of exhaustion, 'reduced efficacy in work' and 'negativism or cynicism related to one's job*'.[46]

For workers at the COVID frontline, already demanding occupations became newly hazardous, stricken work conditions only exacerbated. For women, finishing one highly stressed job only to come home to another would have pushed many to the brink.

Women's reproductive' work remains a primary focus for feminist theory and is also central to degrowth and gift economy discourses, where it is flagged as a hidden 'gift' which although underpinning growth capitalism, remains assiduously ignored in calculations of GDP, in the same way the gifts—costs—of the natural environment are erased. As Kallis et al. explain, 'growth is … subsidized and sustained by invisible reproductive work in the household'. It is this 'foundational economy' of gendered care works that thus looms large in the mission to decolonise the growth imaginary and to forge pathways out of capitalism.[47]

That women's emotional burden skyrocketed during COVID is well-documented and can only have contributed to bullying cultures of paid work.[48,49] However, the 'toxic' workplaces experienced by Australian of women during 2020 and 2021 must also be seen in a broader cultural context, a culture already noted for its significant, even systemic, sexism.

Sadly, the snowballing polycrises of modern capitalism suggest that work conditions may never fully recover from COVID. A 2022 PwC survey of over 50,000 workers from 44 countries and territories, identified that the '*great resignation*' remains very much alive even after most pandemic restrictions have wound down, with one-in-five survey respondents reporting they were considering a job change in the coming year.[50] While low wages remain a factor driving discontent for 75% of workers, finding '*fulfilment*' at work was also important, with 66% of people seeking opportunities to 'truly be themselves' at work.

In Australia, we see '*a gendered version of the Great Resignation happening*'.[51] We have an education sector characterised by 'last ditch' strikes and worker exodus, and a devastated rural healthcare network, with women '*resigning in droves in the middle of a pandemic … driven by chronic underpayment and overwork* [and] *the high cost of childcare*.[52] In urban areas, nurses' '*desire for better conditions and upwards mobility*' has seen a sharp increase of workdays lost to industrial disputes, in an 'indisputable' sign that workers are increasingly prepared to challenge the status quo. In the December 2022, 40.5% of total working days lost in Australia were in the education and training, and healthcare and social assistance industries.[53]

Worker movements, some seismic shifts, show how the pandemic continues to reshape working culture. Some believe the crisis may help to shift the balance of power from employers to employees, rewriting '*the psychological contract between employers and employees ... the deal you make with your employer about what you get in exchange for your labour, time and effort*'.[54] This is however, only likely to be a temporary blip in a global growth economy that functions so very like the Ponzi scheme example, sucking resources from the bottom up until the well is dry.

'Corporate Feminism'

In Australia and across the globe, gender inequalities and other injustices permeate every sphere of life. Even in the upper echelons of the corporate world, old boys' networks still dominate, driving the enduring gender pay gap and workplace harassment.[55] In Australia, unequal pay is just one manifestation of a social order in which women are - relatively - marginalised.[56]

While frustrating for those banging on the corporate glass ceiling, in the more visceral context of women working at the lower end of the economic scale, it is hard to sympathise with these perhaps more liberal or corporate feminists, the individualised, 'lean in' philosophies of top earners such as Facebook's Sheryl Sandberg which largely neglect the intersectional and systemic discrimination faced by other women.[57]

The typical representation of 'gender equality' in Australia is characterised by white and well-educated women who want to 'achieve big'. The advocacy around this naturally falls into the language of female 'leadership', encouragement into 'STEM' subjects at school and greater participation in sports. It is effectively a marketing exercise for liberalism, because the onus is on individuals *to just try harder*, ignoring the patri-colonial hierarchical structures still churning in the background. Indeed, evidence shows that an increase in women 'business leaders', has little real impact upon gender inequity beyond the individuals concerned: i.e., it is personal promotion disguised as feminism.[58]

Sadly, the price of this increased gender equality of well-educated, (typically white) women, is whole industries of working class (often foreign) women workers brought in to do the domestic work which supports their 'liberation'. These domestic workers, usually women from the countries of the global South, often have to relinquish the gift of raising their own family for another woman's family, to ensure they earn enough. Although not as typical to Australia as to the US, financial remittances from women's imported domestic labour makes up *a third of the GDP* of some countries, for example, in The Caribbean.[59]

Across the globe, economic inequality remains a key and systemic driver of gender disadvantage for women. In Australia, women are more reliant on 'welfare' payments, more likely to be employed in insecure jobs, and most vulnerable to any austerity measures that may arise from the pandemic ashes.[60]

COVID has not increased the bargaining rights of Australian workers—our challenges remain the same, if not exacerbated.[61]

The 'great resignation' narrative works in the same way, hiding the commonality of deteriorating work conditions to instead speak to individual choice and the privilege inherent to many 'antiwork' tactics.[62] While sometimes hailed as 'a kind of spontaneous, informal labour strike', 'the closest thing we've seen in a century to a general strike'; with a dearth of co-ordination these 'movements' are perhaps really only *sentiments*, an expression of individualised control but powerless as an anti-capitalist 'exit' strategy:[63]

> The Great Resignation discourse does little more than reveal the limitations of labour movements, and their distance from the material realities of life under capitalism that are the primary focus of working-class movements … This is particularly true in Australia.[64]

From Antiwork to Degrowth

Writing at the height of the pandemic, Susan Paulson tells us:

> The crisis we face as a global community must be understood not only as a public health crisis, or as an economic crisis of the capitalist mode of production, but also, fundamentally, as a crisis of the reproduction of life. In this sense, it is a crisis of care: the work of caring for humans, non-humans, and the shared biosphere. The pandemic is a historical rupture.[65]

As noted in the introductory chapter to this book, the concept of degrowth seemed to gain a much wider audience, if not genuine traction, as a result of the coronavirus crisis. For Paulson and other degrowth philosophers, the principles at the heart of degrowth must have an anticapitalist message if they are to address the cascading transgressions of the growth paradigm. The 'open letter' noted in chapter one was successful in attracting so many signatures because of a growing understanding of the urgent need to:

1. Put life at the centre of our economic systems, not economic growth;
2. Radically re-evaluate how much and what work is necessary for a good life for all, emphasising care work;
3. Organise society around the provision of essential goods and services, minimising wasteful practices;
4. Democratise societies, struggling against authoritarian and technocratic tendencies;
5. Base political and economic systems on the principle of solidarity, rather than competition and greed.[66]

Sadly however, we have a very long way to go.

In This Chapter ...

We have seen how antiwork movements provide evidence of worker dissatisfaction, but also the lack of worker capacity to organise in collective ways/actions to tackle the dis-ease so common to modern workplaces; both during the pandemic and more broadly: the zeitgeist of late-stage capitalism.

In the Next Chapter ...

We will consider whether the learnings from the two studies of women's work during the pandemic, one depicting the businesses of care capitalism and the other, a female-led gift economy model, offer us hope still for a degrowth future.

Notes

1. Stanford, J. (2016). Manufacturing (Still) Matters: Why the Decline of Australian Manufacturing is NOT Inevitable, and What Government Can Do About It. The Australia Institute Briefing Paper. https://australiainstitute.org.au/wp-content/uploads/2020/12/Manufacturing-Briefing-Paper-FINAL.pdf. Accessed March 2020.
2. Gilfillan, G. and McGann, C. (2018). Trends in union membership in Australia. Parliament of Australia.https://www.aph.gov.au/About_Parliament/Parliamentary_Departments/Parliamentary_Library/pubs/rp/rp1819/UnionMembership. Accessed May 2020.
3. Stansfield, E. (2020). Topic of contention: Casualisation of the workforce. UNSW Newsroom, July 1, 2020. https://newsroom.unsw.edu.au/news/business-law/topic-contention-casualisation-workforce. Accessed March 2021.
4. Duckett, S. (2020). Commentary: The Consequences of Private Involvement in Healthcare – The Australian Experience. Health Policy, May 2020. 15(4): 21–25. doi: https://doi.org/10.12927/hcpol.2020.26228.
5. Kiely, R. (2003). The race to the bottom and international labor solidarity. *Review (Fernand Braudel Center)*, 67–88.
6. Warren, K. (2016). Rise of gig economy threatens vulnerable workers. *Newsmonth*, *36*(7), 5.
7. Australian Bureau of Statistics. (2020). Casuals hardest hit by job losses in 2020. https://www.abs.gov.au/media-centre/media-releases/casuals-hardest-hit-job-losses-2020. Accessed March 2021.
8. Australian Bureau of Statistics. (2020). Working arrangements. https://www.abs.gov.au/statistics/labour/earnings-and-working-conditions/working-arrangements/aug-2020. Accessed March 2021.
9. Gilfillan, G. and McGann, C. (Australian Bureau of Statistics). (2018). https://www.abs.gov.au/articles/insights-casual-employment-occupation-and-industry 15 October 2018. Accessed May 2021.
10. Afshar, V. (2020). Are you working at home or sleeping at work? *ZDNet Business.* May 20, 2020. https://www.zdnet.com/article/are-you-working-at-home-or-sleeping-at-work/. Accessed Feb 2021.
11. Naughton, J. (2020). Working from home was the dream but is it turning into a nightmare? The Guardian. Aug 15, 2020. https://www.theguardian.com/commentisfree/2020/aug/15/working-from-home-was-the-dream-but-is-it-turning-into-a-nightmare. Accessed Aug 2021.
12. Training Industry. (2020). Are We Working From Home or Sleeping at the Office? Training Industry, Nov 21, 2020. https://trainingindustry.com/articles/remote-learning/are-we-working-from-home-or-sleeping-at-the-office-spon-commlabindia/. Accessed Aug 2021.

13. For a complete list of lockdown dates see: https://www.platinumaccounting.com.au/melbourne-lockdown-dates/.
14. City of Melbourne. (2023). Strong return of office workers to Melbourne's CBD. *Melbourne News*, March 5, 2023. https://news.melbourne.vic.gov.au/media-releases/strong-return-of-office-workers-to-melbournes-cbd/. Accessed March 2023.
15. CFI Co. (2022). Working from Home, or Living at Work? Hybrid is 'Hell', and a Return to Office may be Worse CFI.co - Capital Finance International. July 28, 2023. https://cfi.co/brave-new-world/2022/07/working-from-home-or-living-at-work-hybrid-is-hell-and-a-return-to-office-may-be-worse/. Accessed Aug 2022.
16. Ricketts, L. R. and Rogers, W. M. (2022). The Great Retirement: Who Are the Retirees? The Economy Blog. Jan 4, 2022. https://www.stlouisfed.org/on-the-economy/2022/january/great-retirement-who-are-retirees. Accessed Jan 2022.
17. Dill, K. (2021). America's Workers Are Leaving Jobs in Record Numbers. Wall Street Journal, Oct 15, 2021. https://www.wsj.com/articles/whats-driving-americas-workers-to-leave-jobs-in-record-numbers-11634312414?mod=Searchresults_pos8&page=1. Accessed Feb 2022.
18. Regional Australia Institute. (2022). Regional Movers Index report found migration from capital cities to regional Australia increased by 16.6% during the 2021/22 financial year when lockdowns occurred. https://regionalaustralia.org.au/Web/Web/Toolkits-Indexes/Regional-Movers-Index.aspx. Accessed March 2022.
19. Carroll, A., Forrest, K., Sanders-O'Connor, E., Flynn, L., Bower, J. M., Fynes-Clinton, S., & Ziaei, M. (2022). Teacher stress and burnout in Australia: examining the role of intrapersonal and environmental factors. *Social Psychology of Education*, *25*(2–3), 441–469.
20. Daniel, E., & Van Bergen, P. (2023). Teacher burnout during COVID-19: associations with instructional self-efficacy but not emotion regulation. *Teachers and Teaching*, 1–19.
21. Dobson, H., Malpas, C. B., Burrell, A. J., Gurvich, C., Chen, L., Kulkarni, J., & Winton-Brown, T. (2021). Burnout and psychological distress amongst Australian healthcare workers during the COVID-19 pandemic. *Australasian Psychiatry*, *29*(1), 26–30.
22. Shine, K., (2015). Reporting the 'exodus': News coverage of teacher shortage in Australian newspapers. *Issues in Educational Research*, *25*(4), pp. 501–516. Australia's 'mass exodus' of workers in the education and care work sectors.
23. Picci, A. (Undated). Crying on the job? You're not alone, with 8 in 10 workers shedding tears. CBS Money Watch. https://www.cbsnews.com/news/crying-on-the-job-youre-not-alone-with-8-in-10-workers-shedding-tears/. Accessed March 2023.

24. Greenslade, L., McAuliffe, D., & Chenoweth, L. (2015). Social workers' experiences of covert workplace activism. *Australian Social Work*, *68*(4), 422–437.
25. Lloyd, C., & King, R. (2004). A survey of burnout among Australian mental health occupational therapists and social workers. *Social psychiatry and psychiatric epidemiology*, *39*, 752–757.
26. Olley, R. (2023). Hear me, see me, trust you–job burnout and disengagement of Australian aged care workers. *Leadership in Health Services*, *36*(1), 111–124.
27. Stack Exchange. (Undated). https://english.stackexchange.com/questions/605221/when-did-the-expression-hustle-culture-emerge. Accessed April 2023.
28. Balkeran, A. (2020). Hustle culture and the implications for our workforce.
29. McGregor, G. (2022). Before 'quiet quitting' in the U.S., there was 'lying flat' in China. How the anti-work movement swept the world's two largest economies. Fortune Magazine, Sept 2, 2022. https://tinyurl.com/4mjcw6n8. Accessed Oct 2022. Also cited in https://www.investopedia.com/what-is-quiet-quitting-6743910; Accessed Oct 2022.
30. Brossard, M. (2022). Lying flat: Profiling the 'tangping' attitude. *Made in China Journal*, *7*(2), pp. 50–63.
31. Tan, J.S. (2022). Tech Workers Lie Flat. Dissent, 69(2), pp. 32–41.
32. Filev, A. (2022). The Hot Potato Effect: How it impacts workflow. Forbes. https://www.forbes.com/sites/andrewfilev/2022/07/28/the-hot-potato-effect-how-it-impacts-workflows/?sh=63d1d6924e55. Accessed Oct 2022.
33. Filev, A. (2022). Ibid.
34. Molina, O. (2023). Hustle Culture: The Toxic Impact on Mental Health. Talkspace, Feb 20, 2023. https://www.talkspace.com/blog/hustle-culture/#:~:text=Culture%20with%20Talkspace-,What%20is%20hustle%20culture%3F,levels%2C%20burnout%2C%20and%20depression. Accessed Feb 2023.
35. Hunt, E. (2022). Rage rooms and primal screams: how stressed-out workers are letting off steam. The Guardian, Sept 24, 2022. https://www.theguardian.com/lifeandstyle/2022/sep/23/rage-rooms-and-primal-screams-how-stressed-out-workers-are-letting-off-steam. Accessed Sept 2022.
36. Ibid.
37. Ibid.
38. The Reddit online community is described as a "A subreddit for those who want to end work, are curious about ending work, want to get the most out of a work-free life, want more information on anti-work ideas and want personal help with their own jobs/work-related struggles".
39. Tobotic. (2021). r/Antiwork Survey Results. Reddit, Dec 5, 2021. https://antiwork.uk/2021/12/05/r-antiwork-survey-results/#gender. Accessed Jan 2022.

40. Tobotic. (2021). Ibid.
41. Cesran International. (2017). Neoliberalism and the Social Contract: A Historical Perspective. Cesran Blog, Dec 16, 2017. Accessed Oct 2022.
42. Griffiths, E. (2019) Why Are Young People Pretending to Love Work? New York Times, Jan 26, 2019. https://www.nytimes.com/2019/01/26/business/against-hustle-culture-rise-and-grind-tgim.html. Accessed Jan 2022.
43. Tobotic. (2021). Ibid.
44. Statistica. (2022). Regional distribution of desktop traffic to Reddit.com as of May 2022 by country https://www.statista.com/statistics/325144/reddit-global-active-user-distribution/. Accessed Oct 2022.
45. Dixon, S. (2022). Reddit: distribution of global audiences 2022, by gender: Statistica, Mar 22, 2022. https://www.statista.com/statistics/1255182/distribution-of-users-on-reddit-worldwide-gender/.
46. World Health Organisation. (2019). Burn-out an "occupational phenomenon": International Classification of Diseases. https://www.who.int/news/item/28-05-2019-burn-out-an-occupational-phenomenon-international-classification-of-diseases. Accessed Oct 2020.
47. Kallis, G., Demaria, F., and D'Alisa, G. (Eds.) (2014). Introduction of Degrowth: A Vocabulary for a New Era. Routledge. DOIhttps://doi.org/10.4324/9780203796146.
48. Australian Bureau of Statistics. (2021). Household Impacts of Covid 19 Survey, Feb 2021. https://www.abs.gov.au/methodologies/household-impacts-covid-19-survey-methodology/feb-2021. Accessed April 2021.
49. Australian National University. (2020). Worry increases, distancing decreases with COVID second wave. https://www.anu.edu.au/news/all-news/worry-increases-distancing-decreases-with-covid-second-wave. Accessed April 2021.
50. PwC. (2022). ibid. https://www.pwc.com/gx/en/issues/workforce/hopes-and-fears-2022.html.
51. Zola, D. (2022). The Great Resignation: an Australian perspective. Overland. March 22, 2022. https://overland.org.au/2022/03/the-great-resignation-an-australian-perspective/. Accessed April 2022.
52. Zola, D. (2022). The Great Resignation: an Australian perspective. Overland. March 22, 2022. https://overland.org.au/2022/03/the-great-resignation-an-australian-perspective/. Accessed April 2022.
53. Australian Bureau Statistics. (2023). Industrial Disputes, Australia. Reference period December 2022. https://www.abs.gov.au/statistics/labour/earnings-and-work-hours/industrial-disputes-australia/latest-release. Accessed Feb 2023.
54. Calder, R. (2022). Has the great resignation actually happened in Australia? *Australian Institute of Training & Development*, *49*(1), pp.40–42. https://search.informit.org/doi/abs/10.3316/informit.453315890177066.

55. The Strait Times. (2021). An unapologetic Old Boys' network is costing Australia billions, Oct 21, 2021. https://www.straitstimes.com/asia/australianz/an-unapologetic-old-boys-network-is-costing-australia-billions. Accessed Oct 2021.
56. Workplace Gender Equality Agency (2022). Australia's Gender Equality Scorecard Key results from the Workplace Gender Equality Agency's Employer Census 2021–22. WGEA-Gender-Equality-Scorecard-2022.
57. Ng, E. and Stanton, P. (2023). The great resignation: managing people in a post COVID-19 pandemic world. Personnel Review, 52(2), pp.401–407. https://doi.org/10.1108/PR-03-2023-914.
58. Livingstone, E. (2016). 'Corporate feminism' oppresses women. Here's how. The Guardian, Sept 28, 2016. https://www.theguardian.com/commentisfree/2016/sep/28/corporate-feminism-women-glass-ceiling Accessed Jan 2020.
59. Antrobus, P. (2004) The Disaster: The Gift and Caribbean Economics. Women's World conference. Ottawa. Audio transcript: http://gift-economy.com/a-radically-different-world-view-is-possible/. Accessed Jan 2021.
60. Gender and Development Network. (2018). The impact of austerity on women. Submission to the Independent Expert on Foreign Debt, March 2018. https://www.ohchr.org/sites/default/files/Documents/Issues/Development/IEDebt/WomenAusterity/GenderDevelopmentNetwork.pdf. Accessed April 2019.
61. Hannam, P. (2021). Australian workers have more bargaining power post-lockdowns, ACTU says. The Guardian, Nov 11, 2021. https://www.theguardian.com/business/2021/nov/11/australian-workers-have-more-bargaining-power-post-lockdowns-actu-says. Accessed Dec 2021.
62. Press, A. (2022). Why Are US Workers Quitting Their Jobs in Droves? Jacobin. Jan 25, 2022. https://jacobin.com/2022/01/us-white-collar-workers-quitting-nytimes-quitagion-great-resignation
63. New York Times. (2021). Could the Great Resignation Help Workers? Take a Look at History. NYT, Dec 12, 2021. https://www.nytimes.com/2021/12/11/opinion/great-resignation-labor-shortage.html. Accessed Jan 2022.
64. Zola, D. (2022). The Great Resignation: an Australian perspective. Overland, March 22, 2022. https://overland.org.au/2022/03/the-great-resignation-an-australian-perspective/. Accessed April 2022.
65. Paulson, S. (2020). Degrowth and feminisms ally to forge care-full paths beyond pandemic. Interface: *A journal for and about social movements.* Movement report Volume 12 (1): 232–246 (July 2020). https://www.interfacejournal.net/wp-content/uploads/2020/07/Interface-12-1-Paulson.pdf. Accessed Jan 2021.
66. Ibid.

CHAPTER 11

A Degrowth Reality

Abstract This concluding chapter draws together the themes of previous chapters. With the typical modern Australian workplace a social construct reflecting of neoliberal culture, the author argues that work becomes increasingly risky not only for women workers, but for the many other cohorts who are deprivileged within the pyramid of capital, particularly those with intersecting traits which make them more vulnerable to structural disadvantage. The scars of neoliberal economic fundamentalism, combined with the fresher wounds of the COVID crisis, have particularly impacted the highly commodified and female-dominated care frontline. That harmful, and even traumatic experiences can routinely occur in the course of one's paid employment is never acceptable. That 'the toxic workplace' appears to be endemic to Australia needs urgent investigation and systemic remediation. In contrast, the interactions and practices recorded in *The Gift Highway* study show that the activities of (women) 'workers' in hyperlocal online workspaces instead exhibit the tenets of degrowth theory: open localism, reciprocity, conviviality and a decolonising of the growth imaginary. In showing that a gift economy model operating mostly outside of market capitalism rewards women workers in multiple ways, offers genuine hope for transformative change.

M. Jordan, *Women's Work in the Pandemic Economy*,
https://doi.org/10.1007/978-3-031-40154-1_11

Keywords Capitalism • Pyramid of capital • Degrowth • Polycrises • Care • Labour • Gender • Horizontalism • Collectivism • Masculinity • Labour • Gender

Introduction

This concluding chapter draws together the themes and reasonings of previous chapters. It shows that 'the workplace', as a social construct of neoliberal Australian culture, is increasingly risky for many women workers, and for other labour cohorts who are deprivileged within the pyramid of capital.

The psychological hazards experienced by over half of women participating in the *Generation Expendable?* study, suggest that bullying, workload burden and worker burnout are *endemic* to the businesses of care in Australia and not specific to the coronavirus pandemic. The factors underpinning 'the toxic workplace' so frequently described by respondents sadly continue to impact significantly both on workers, and often, their care recipients.

In addition to increased workplace stressors during the coronavirus crisis, many women also experienced a sharp rise in demand at home. Typically, this included the home schooling of primary and secondary school children and managing additional housework as partners started working remotely and adult children moved home. In addition, shouldering the emotional load for one's immediate and often also extended family meant that many women's own health suffered. The pressures across 2020 and 2021 even for those women who *hadn't* lost or relinquished work were enormous. For many, they still resonate.

The pink recession initially flagged in the first months of Australia's pandemic had predicted long-term financial impacts for women, as many lost the independence and security of paid employment. The shift of so many adult workers into the home 'office' also exposed women to a new, or greatly increased vulnerability to intimate partner violence.

At work, this increased risk of violence also manifested, albeit mainly psychological harm. The commonality of toxic workplace cultures and practices that women reported in *Generation Expendable?* exposes deeply rooted problems in Australian workplace cultures, cultures which expressly disempower and devalue workers through structures of competition and hierarchy which were designed in with colonisation and settlement and endure still.

The scars of the economic fundamentalism of late-stage capitalism combined with the fresher wound of the COVID crisis, have particularly impacted the commodified and feminised care frontline. That harmful, and even traumatic experiences of workplace bullying occur in the course of one's paid employment is never acceptable. That 'the toxic workplace' appears to be endemic in Australia needs urgent investigation and systemic remediation.

To move beyond our current modes of social and economic organisation, to relearn or to reapply *relational* models of working, of caring for humanity and for our planet more broadly, we have to look at the heuristic settings of our behaviour; at economic—social—behaviours across the board. This may not be as difficult as it seems. Degrowth theory, decolonial feminisms, antiwork movements and other loosely aligned anti- or postcapitalist thinking shows us that transformative change *is* possible.

Current models of labour and work are failing women and other non-'masculated' genders, including the many men who are already engaging in 'other-oriented', and thus female-coded practices, such as those identified engaging with the Good Karma Effect gift economy model. With a pluriverse of Indigenous, gift economy and even what might be described as 'matriarchal' practices enduring in under pandemic conditions, it is clear that socio-economic systems which hinge on a GDP definition of growth, on self-reward and material excess, can be effectively and even pragmatically defied.

The New (COVID) Normal

Australians rallied during the coronavirus crisis. At the peak of the pandemic, social cohesion rose 'quite significantly', according to the Scanlon Foundation.[1] This is attributable to several factors—not least to a policy of furlough for employed people unable to work, and meaningful financial support for those on government ('welfare') payments or and experiencing homelessness.

Early rhetoric that Australians were '*all in this together*' didn't, however, endure. Even before vaccination programs were well established, many pandemic supports had been rolled back and talk of (government) debt management, including potential austerity measures known to predominantly disadvantage women, were materialising.[2,3,4,5,6]

Three years on, the zeitgeist has definitively shifted. The latest Scanlon Social Cohesion Survey shows that Australians' 'sense of national pride', 'sense of social justice' and 'sense of belonging', all now sit at a lower point than *before* the pandemic. The crisis has exposed insecurities, risks and even existential hazards beyond the bounds of the virus itself, the real and present dangers of our resolutely neoliberal, 'growth' capitalism: an economic paradigm of destruction and excess in which a parasitic global North still feeds off a supposedly postcolonial global South.

Hierarchies of value that were structured in at the time of Australia's invasion and settlement still resonate broadly across our national culture. Binaries of what is 'normal' and what is 'other', including the gender dichotomy, can be seen to still shape Australia's institutions of both work and of home in essential ways signalling that the patriarchal colonial mission which exported capitalism across the globe is not historical, but a very real and *present danger*, as evidenced by enduring misogyny, even in the country's workplaces of government.

That the economic fallout from the pandemic was so strongly gendered exposes the systemic vulnerabilities that women still face in twenty-first-century Australia. Disadvantage and discrimination, particularly for women with intersecting identity traits of race, disability and so on, see Australian women increasingly exposed to poverty in older age—in one of the wealthiest countries in the world. It also tells us that without addressing these issues, women will be far less (financially) resilient to the increasingly inevitable cascade of polycrises of late-stage capitalism.

While this book has focused on a universalised experience of (female) gender, it is unquestionable that women of colour, women with disability or chronic health conditions, single-income women and single mothers, LGBIQA+ Australians, and most expressly First Nations women, face far greater exposure to structural discrimination: social determinants intrinsically linked to socio-economic status and therefore life outcomes.

As Genevieve Vaughan and other gift economy advocates tell us, human behaviour is now fundamentally shaped within the context of capitalism:

> Our society is now based on exchange. And the logic of exchange is validated everywhere … influences everything we think and the way we behave. Making us more self-interested and more attached to reflections and judgments about ourselves and others.[7]

Yet this doesn't mean that all our behaviours, particularly ego-oriented 'economic' behaviours focused on individual advance is fixed and immutable, as the findings of *The Gift Highway* show. Outside of the hierarchical structures and intense pressures of paid employment, we saw a very different model of women's labour/behaviour in collectively provisioning care.

In the example of Naarm-based Good Karma Networks, we recorded members of hyper-local digital territories responding to place-based needs in real time; gifting, (re)gifting and sharing often scarce material goods; communities—micro gift economies—where members were routinely engaging in both material and non-material gifting practices: sharing positive, useful and humorous stories, gifting empathic and care-full advice, taking time to post up-to-date information and to respond to the often urgently expressed needs of their fellow human beings in collective and 'hive mind' ways.

The interactions and practices recorded in *The Gift Highway* show hyperlocal communities, really *workplaces*, enacting core tenets of degrowth theory: with open localism, reciprocity and conviviality all evident, albeit functioning unknowingly, i.e. outside of any theoretical or political context.

That the predominantly female membership of the GKNs so readily engaged in activities of gifting, in provisioning and responding to need in ways that sit outside of the competitive exchange logic of market capitalism, offers potential, and even genuine hope, that an urgently needed *decolonising of the growth imaginary* can and will transpire.

The study of the GKE model revealed online environments which, rather than rewarding 'profit' or quid pro quo reciprocity, actually encouraged economic behaviours that were both *other-focused* and care-full, recreating and reinforcing the sense of belonging and connection to community stalwartly disincentivised within the fragmented consumerism of growth capitalism.

With value hierarchies so deeply embedded into Australian culture, that the design of virtual spaces allows users to construct/deconstruct whatever 'identity' they like may be important. The facility of constructing an online persona is of course best known for negative associations, such as 'catfishing' or other fraudulent activities. In looking to further psychological processes of decolonisation however, to perhaps drive a universalisation of identity/humanity through the removal of visual cues linked to (negative) stereotyping and so forth, virtual communities may have unrecognised potential.

While a more purposeful process of dismantling the value propositions inherent to patri-colonial capitalism might be ideal, practices which even *accidentally* work to increase inclusion through interaction with the 'other' still hold potential in opening up social relationships and from there, hopefully seeding familiarity, understanding and acceptance of difference in ways which, like more typical economic behaviours, eventually become axiomatically repetitive and from there, can cumulate in enduringly positive ways.

Whilst the paid workplaces of pandemic caregiving were imploding, the micro gift economies of Good Karma were literally spreading their eponymous message; their predominantly female membership convivially engaged in other-focused, empathetic and care-full communications.

Mariam Abazeri explains the vital role of degrowth practice in decolonising, and of decolonising to postcapitalism:

> How do we build coalitions through difference, inhabiting spaces of multiplicity while engaging with the coloniality of power? A space of alternatives to the global capitalist order is a space in which the process of decolonization is underway, resisting and reimaging life beyond neocolonial modernity. It is a space where self-realization can be experienced in many forms, including as an inward journey; where a communal sense of self can be understood as one of several ways we are in relation; where a future of conviviality and equality includes reparative address for past injustices … visibilizing and reimagining other epistemes and ways of constituting ourselves and our habitats.[8]

The gifting interactions of the GKNs definitively had something of a 'maternal', or at least female-coded, element. Not simply in their having attracted a largely female membership, but also in the caring and gifting nature of community interactions, so very different to the individualist and ego-centric dynamisms of the paid workplace. Typically described as 'feminine' behaviours, these are of course not biologically elemental to women, but *socially* constructed. As such, they can be adopted, celebrated and reproduced by any individual, of any gender, in any society, given the right environmental/economic settings.

The Gift Highway study also revealed what might be interpreted as an emergent 'feminisation' of men, not only in their participating in activities of sharing and recycling (gifting), but also in the example of the GKN area with a notably higher and young male demographic, their evident easiness in offering gifts of care and nurture coded 'maternal' in patriarchal discourse.

The contrast between women delivering paid care services, and women volunteering convivial practices and relationships that the two studies detailed, provides a palpable repudiation of gender essentialism. Worker behaviour which might be framed as innate female competitiveness, or 'bitchiness', was shown to be much more common to *masculated* work environments, where male-coded architypes of (individualised) leadership, decision-making and problem solving are still the norm. Workplace cultures characterised by the domination of subordinate or subaltern identities and reproduced structurally through their hierarchal and linear organisation, through entrenched and still masked patri-colonial values, and through the weaponisation of truth and of lying.

Generation Expendable? showed that, instead of coming together to resolve issues and share their pandemic anxieties, women workers both demonstrated and *replicated* work values of competition, 'efficiency' and individualised decision-making, precepts that were structured in well-prior to the pandemic, but which undoubtedly functioned to heighten toxic workplace practices and cultures for workers.

Left to self-organise their care provisioning, women acted very differently. Outside of Australia's commodified and itemised care standard, with its top-down and de-personalised ethos of caregiving as a series of tasks as opposed to trustful relationships, women intuitively worked in the collaborative and care-full ways we see depicted in degrowth 'imaginaries'; the collectivism of the GKE model encouraging material and non-material generosity, shared problem solving and decision-making, and most importantly, what might be described as more natural, logic human behaviours of mutuality in a gift-giving culture. In this gift economy model, both women *and men* were able to express vulnerability without fear of punishment, and from there, to open themselves up to receiving and giving, the regenerative and nurturing social relations that Australia's typical paid workplaces seem to often lack.

A Degrowth Imaginary

Capitalism is a complex system.[9] While ostensibly it speaks only to economic relations, in its 'late' or 'pandemic' stage, the exchange paradigm is marred by polycrises of destruction that expose the pyramidic, even Ponzi-style contradictions of infinite growth.

Mariam Abazeri explains:

> Interstructural effects on social life, relations, activities, in-situations and expectations … A logic that surpasses questions of labor, modes of resistance and recreation that only focus on labor exploitation, and the workplace will fail to dislodge the encompassing force of capital.[10]

That a 'sisterhood' of humanity was found to be thriving even under pandemic conditions, provide some hope—and indeed evidence—that a 'degrowth reset', one encompassing 'feminine'/Indigenous/circular ways of living and interacting already exists, even if outside of activist and academic epistemes. It shows us that a 'decolonisation of the growth imaginary may yet map us a 'gift highway' towards the sustainable, post-capital future so urgently needed.

Horizontal Collectivism

In the micro gift economies of the GKE model, we saw that even a single power tier insufficiently checked, inevitably functions to distinguish self from other, better from lesser. Even with good intentions, and situated 'beyond money', Sandra's story exposed the ways in which any notion of authority can invite misuse and top-down pressure. As a genuine template for degrowth therefore, the GKNs might be enhanced by introducing a more distributive moderation, with administrators regularly rotated to discourage any burnout or overreach of power.

The structures of patriarchal capitalism both create and reproduce 'gender'. Properly described, these are but one of a multitude of value propositions dispersed throughout the pyramid of capital, rendering subaltern identities less powerless and thus in competition, not only for access to privilege, but often tussling for even basic human rights in a white noise of public debate which only obscures the real powers at play.

Demasculating Men

Maternal gift advocate Genevieve Vaughan describes women as 'masculated' by patriarchal culture. I have argued this is evidenced in the so-called liberal feminisms of 'girl boss' corporate capitalism, which values particular (groups of) women over others. This tells us that mainstream 'first world' feminism essentially functions as a product of a larger economic system with little genuine imperative to address social inequality either as it relates to gender, class or other constructs of difference, or to the ongoing and gendered practices of colonisation in global South countries.

Certainly, the studies presented here do little to challenge assertions that patriarchal capitalism purposely invisibilises alternative gift economy labours, which include the unpaid care work of the private sphere as well as the 'gift' of Earth's extracted natural resources, both of which go unrecognised in representations of national wealth and 'growth'.

Just as male workers are rewarded for showing strength, aggression, domination; so too are women still policing the moral economy of capitalism; moral arbiters of (feminine) behaviour who are rewarded by in their fortifying of extant workplace relations.[11] Equally, Australian men are also still routinely 'punished' or diminished when expressing nurturing and caring behaviours.

We can understand from both the studies presented here that constructions of gender and other embodied identities play a fundamental role in perpetuating and safeguarding growth capitalism. They are as essential to the status quo as government policies which resolutely exclude the environments costs of 'the economy' and ignore women's voluntary contributions; the social glue that holds communities together as much as any rule of law.

Outside of constraints of Australia's brusque, and masculated national (work) culture, men quite willingly engage in gifting practices coded 'maternal', or feminine. This tells us that, as with women, if men and boys are given time, opportunity and liberation from an exhaustingly performative masculinity, they also quite *naturally* adopt and adapt to collaborative formations of decision-making, sharing and responding to vulnerability, developing caring connections with other people, with place and with the natural environment.

As Vaughan and other feminists tell us, it is men who are gendered, with masculinity a social construct which operationalises power and control. So it is not only women workers who must be de-masculated, but *also men* who need to be supported and encouraged to move beyond an egocentric and profit-focused 'rational man', to (re)learn and prioritise the other-focused practices—*behavioural heuristics*—of gift economy logic.

A Degrowth Reality

While degrowth advocates continue to develop models and strategies based upon real human values, on collectively-governed and open local communities characterised by care-full and convivial relationships, the findings presented here suggest these might already exist.

In strategising pathways towards degrowth, Susan Paulson suggests:

> A good first move is to foster mutual learning and nourishment among interlocutors and collaborators in qualitatively different positions and places … to heighten awareness of relations of power and difference among us. That means explicitly addressing concerns not only that degrowth activists and thinkers might be co-opted by powerful forces, but also that degrowth processes might co-opt or encompass other visions and pathways.[12]

With the pandemic still wreaking havoc across many areas of Australian life, it has more sharply brought into focus the foundational nature and indeed *power* of caregifting.

The gift economy behaviours recorded in *The Gift Highway*, what I identify as an emergent degrowth, suggest we are not yet irretrievably removed from pre-modern/Indigenous economic models, whether one considers these 'matriarchal' or otherwise. *The Gift Highway* study also illustrates a way in which degrowth advocates might work to decolonise the growth imaginary outside of activism and political philosophy. Important as theory and advocacy are, even anti/postcapitalist activist spaces are often still inclined towards Australian society's deeply engrained notions of competition and fragmentation:

> Many would-be activists and ex-activists … deem anti-capitalists 'utopian' … Frustrated, they critique all sides from the margins or confine themselves to energetically campaigning on single issues. The singularity of separate campaigns within social justice and ecological sustainability spheres leads to competition … All this serves to heighten and deepen fragmentation.[13]

The gifting practices of the GKE model sit consciously outside of politics, and yet within these intentional communities, members routinely enact and re-enact degrowth behaviours. Perhaps therefore, it is time we stopped focusing so energetically on influencing hearts and minds, to also utilise the 'behavioural' sciences, behavioural economics which might tell us that *the more often we practice* (gift-giving), and the *less often* we engage (in exchange capitalism), then very real and human rewards, bounty inherent to the gift economy model, may yet cohere to present a genuine and truly viable alternative to growth capitalism.

As Mariam Abazeri tells us:

> Realization can be experienced in many forms, including as an inward journey; where a communal sense of self can be understood as one of several ways we are in relation; where a future of conviviality and equality … gives way to validation and celebration, visibilizing and reimagining other epistemes and ways of constituting ourselves and our habitats beyond the human/non-human divide.[14]

Similarly, Angela Miles identifies how practices of gift giving offer humanity a *paradigmatic* shift from away growth/death economics:

> We don't just want to fall behind one issue at this time and then the next issue … really we need a political definition or movement … My sense is that this gift paradigm brings us that possibility because [as a] political definition [it] is really deeply, deeply, deeply critical and visionary. It is broad enough and it's deep enough to encompass us and to move us forward and work, I think, in every area.....[15]

As the COVID-19 pandemic rolls on, we cannot wait for others to challenge and disrupt the system. Marta Benavides links our inaction around climate change and social injustice and poverty to 'colonial thinking'.

For Benavides:

> We cannot wait for somebody else to do it … [that] comes from colonialism and internalisation of colonial mentality. That makes us think that we have to leave it for the other.[16]

COVID has rendered the threat of pandemics newly pervasive, an unavoidable by-product of the dis-ease of late-stage capitalism, exposing what Terry Leahy calls '*the ghost in the system*'; narratives and structural dynamics originally disseminated through colonialism, but which continue, driving the gender divide, social inequality and climate disaster.

Real social change can only come from the bottom-up. Small and voluntary initiatives have been shown to be more powerful in driving demonstrable change, as seen in the worker protests currently taking place in

France, and in other examples of resistance to a still dominant patriarchal ideology, such as the #MeToo movement.[17,18]

The pandemic has, at the very least, emphasised an urgent need to rethink our conception of workplace culture and wage labour, most particularly as it presents within the commodification of care. The pandemic has also provided us with evidence of an almost subversive localism, where practices of commoning and gifting underpinned by real human values of social connection and belonging to community thrive against the odds.

This tells us that gift economies are not the 'utopian' post-capitalist solution they are often framed as, but an existent and nonconformist decolonising of the growth imaginary; perhaps even a burgeoning 'information infrastructure' that can be harnessed and built upon through targeted funding and then scaling of models such as the Good Karma Networks.

Angela Miles believes that the paradigm change needed to address the climate disaster is offered by the gift economy model:

> I really have felt there is in the gift paradigm, the theoretical understanding of 'giving', as an alternative paradigm to 'exchange', not just a different type of behaviour: a choice of what we do personally. It really is a distinct[19]

The findings related in this book suggest that a pathway, *a gift highway* to our degrowth future may be hiding in plain sight:

> We need not to invent an abstract utopia to find social structures which would embody the value of motherliness and the practise of gift giving they cause. They have existed over the longest eras of human history. And they still exist worldwide. They have been developed over long historical periods. They embody practical experience and thought gained over millennia, and belong indispensably to the cultural store of knowledge of all humankind. So the most intelligent patterns of social organisation can inspire us and teach us to develop the matriarchal model of the future.[20]

Notes

1. Murphy, K. (2021). Toughing out Covid: how Australia's social fabric held together during a once-in-a-century crisis. The Guardian, Feb 4, 2021). https://www.theguardian.com/australia-news/2021/feb/04/

coronavirus-toughing-out-covid-why-australia-chose-not-to-fracture-during-a-once-in-a-century-crisis. Accessed May 2021.

2. Ticha, V. (2021). Is Australia's coronavirus bill a debt burden future generations must bear? University of NSW. Sep 13, 2021. https://newsroom.unsw.edu.au/news/business-law/australias-coronavirus-bill-debt-burden-future-generations-must-bear. Accessed April 2023.
3. Mizen, R. and O'Mallon, F. (2021). Total Australian state and federal government debt to double to $2trn. Financial Review, June 23, 2021. https://www.afr.com/policy/economy/total-australian-state-and-federal-government-debt-to-double-to-2trn-20210623-p583fz#:~:text=Total%20debt%20held%20by%20Australian,to%20global%20investment%20bank%20UBS.&text=Commonwealth%20net%20debt%20is%20expected,of%20GDP%20in%20June%202,025. Accessed July 2022.
4. Breunig, R, and Rose, T. (2022). Paying back Australia's COVID-19 debt. Tax and Transfer Policy Institute. Crawford School of Public Policy, ANU. https://taxpolicy.crawford.anu.edu.au/sites/default/files/publication/taxstudies_crawford_anu_edu_au/2022-08/complete_rose_breunig_wp_july_2022.pdf. Accessed Aug 2022.
5. Tsiaplias, S., & Wang, J. (2023). The Australian Economy in 2022–23: Inflation and Higher Interest Rates in a Post-COVID-19 World. *Australian Economic Review*, *56*(1), 5–19.
6. Davies, H., & O'Callaghan, C. (2014). All in this together? Feminisms, academia, austerity. *Journal of Gender Studies*, *23*(3), 227–232.
7. Vaughan, G. (2004). Heterosexual economics: gift giving and exchange. The gift economy inside and outside of patriarchal capitalism Nov 12–14, 2004.
8. Abazeri, M. (2022). Decolonial feminisms and degrowth. *Elsevier Journal Futures* 136. (2022). 102,902. p. 5.
9. Klitgaard, K.A. and Krall, L., 2012. Ecological economics, degrowth, and institutional change. *Ecological Economics*, *84*, pp. 247–253.
10. Abazeri, M. (2022). Decolonial feminisms and degrowth. *Elsevier Journal Futures* 136. (2022). 102,902. p. 5.
11. See: Leahy, T. (2022). Liberal Feminism and the Socialist Critique. *System Change Made Simple* podcast, Ep 6, Season 2. https://www.buzzsprout.com/2014361/11246992-liberal-feminism-and-the-socialist-critique. (Accessed Jan 2023).
12. Paulson, S. (2022). Reflections on dynamics of strategy in degrowth. *Degrowth Blog*. https://degrowth.info/en/blog/reflections-on-the-role-and-nature-of-strategy-in-degrowth?s=09. Accessed Nov 2022.
13. Nelson, A. (2022). Beyond Money. Apple Books. p. 417.
14. Abazeri, M. (2022). ibid. p. 5

15. Miles, A. (2007). Women's Giving. A New Frame for Feminist Policy Demands Women and the Gift Economy: A Radically Difference Worldview is Possible. Inanna Publications. p. 364.
16. Benavides, M. (2004). Reflecting on the gift economy and gifting in El Salvador. http://www.gift-economy.com/womenand/womenand_reflecting.html. Accessed Nov 2020.
17. Reeler, D. (2017). Exploring the real work of social change: Seven questions that keep us awake. *Leading and Managing in the Social Sector: Strategies for Advancing Human Dignity and Social Justice*, pp. 57–74.
18. Brady, M., (2020). Why not reform education from the bottom up for a real change. *Blog de Diane Ravitch. 14 de mayo*. Accessed Nov 2020.
19. Miles, A. (2007). Women's Giving. A New Frame for Feminist Policy Demands Women and the Gift Economy: A Radically Difference Worldview is Possible. Inanna Publications. p. 364.
20. Gottner-Abendroth, H. (2004). Matriarchal Society and the Gift Paradigm. Motherliness as an Ethical Principle. http://www.gift-economy.com/womenand/matriarchal%20society.html. Accessed Nov 2020.

Index[1]

NUMBERS AND SYMBOLS
#MeToo, 44

A
Abazeri, Mariam, 50, 154, 156, 159
Aged care, 19, 21, 45, 46, 63, 137
Ageism, 4
Anticapitalism, 142, 143
Antiwork, 135–143, 151
Antrobus, Peggy, 5, 40, 88
Australia, 3, 4, 6, 8, 13n53, 24, 34, 35, 40, 44–46, 49, 50, 56–59, 61, 84, 100, 111, 112, 135–137, 139–142, 145n18, 151, 152, 155, 157
Australian culture, 150
Australian Human Rights Commission (AHRC), 44, 45

B
Belonging, 80, 153, 160
Benavides, Marta, 159
The big lie, 102
Binarism, 109
Biological essentialism, 123
Bonchek, Mark, 48
Burnout, 50, 128, 137, 138, 140–141, 150
Business of caring, 2–9
BuyNothing, 57

C
Capitalism, 2, 5–8, 40, 46–50, 56–58, 65, 67, 82, 83, 87–89, 94, 95, 101, 102, 104, 109–112, 114–116, 122–131, 139, 140, 142, 143, 152–157, 159

[1] Note: Page numbers followed by 'n' refer to notes.

M. Jordan, *Women's Work in the Pandemic Economy*,
https://doi.org/10.1007/978-3-031-40154-1

Care, 4, 5, 7, 8, 17, 18, 21, 26, 27, 40, 45, 46, 50, 56–59, 61–64, 67, 68, 69n15, 74, 83, 84, 86, 88, 89, 96, 101, 111–113, 123, 127, 128, 136, 137, 140, 142, 143, 150, 151, 153, 155, 157, 160
Care frontline, 4, 16, 21, 24, 27, 101, 151
Care-full, 8, 64, 75, 84, 87–89, 127–128, 153–155, 158
Caregiving, 4, 6–8, 34, 48, 51, 56, 57, 62, 63, 68, 74, 78, 154, 155
Carers, 56, 62
Casual, 3, 17, 18, 20, 21, 136, 138
Casualisation, 136
Childcare, 74, 140
Chodorow, Nancy, 110
Circular economy, 129
Climate, 2, 49, 65, 101, 122, 123, 129, 159, 160
Climate crisis, 65
Collective bargaining, 135
Collective provisioning, 62, 79, 81, 83, 153
Collectivism, 111, 155, 156
Colonial legacy, 6, 45
Colonisation, 66, 100, 122, 124, 150, 157
Commodification (of everything), 94, 130
Commoning, 2, 64, 65, 77, 80, 83, 115, 160
The Commons, 115
Communication, 26, 58, 74, 76, 77, 154
Community, 4–6, 19, 28n17, 51, 56, 57, 59, 60, 63–65, 77, 79, 80, 82–84, 88, 89, 95, 96, 100–102, 129, 133n14, 142, 146n38, 153, 154, 157, 158, 160
Community exchange systems (CETS), 57
Competition, 2, 5, 7, 40, 56, 65, 76, 88, 94, 104, 108, 112, 113, 122, 136, 143, 150, 155, 156, 158
Consumerism, 153
Conviviality, 78, 87–89, 95, 96, 153, 154, 159
Coronavirus, 2, 8, 26, 27, 46, 50, 58, 122, 136, 137, 143, 150, 151
Corporate feminism, 109, 111–113, 131, 141–142
Corporatisation, 62, 84
COVID, 2–5, 11n29, 16, 17, 19, 21, 22, 24, 26, 28n3, 34, 35, 40, 45, 46, 56, 57, 59, 61, 63, 64, 67, 68, 69n15, 75, 78, 80, 84, 86, 90n13, 95, 100, 122, 127, 137–140, 142, 151–155, 159
Crisis of care, 142
Cultural myths/narratives, 6, 108
Culture, 2, 5, 6, 16, 23–24, 26, 27, 34–35, 40, 45–47, 49, 50, 56, 58, 62, 66–68, 75, 79, 84, 87, 88, 94, 95, 101, 103, 108, 109, 111, 113, 114, 123–125, 127–129, 136, 138–141, 150, 152, 153, 155–157, 160

D

Decolonise, 49, 100, 114, 140
Degrowth, 2, 3, 5, 7–8, 47–50, 57, 58, 65, 66, 74, 75, 78–80, 83, 84, 86, 87, 89, 95, 100–102, 104, 105n17, 113–115, 122, 125, 128, 130, 131, 140, 142–143, 150–160
Democracy, 6, 79
Democratic, 115, 129
Deunionisation, 112, 131
Digital-economy, 5
Disability/chronic condition, 5, 16, 17, 38, 87, 152

Discrimination, 22, 44, 45, 141, 152
Dolmetsch, Andrea, 124
Domestic burden, 3
Dual discriminations, 4, 22
Dual income, 123

E
Ecofeminism, 2, 114
Economic fundamentalism, 7, 46, 151
Economy, 5–8, 19, 44–51, 55, 56, 58, 62, 64–66, 68, 74–89, 94, 95, 99, 100, 102, 108–116, 125, 130, 136, 138, 140, 141, 143, 151–160
Education, 4, 19–20, 27n1, 28n17, 34, 45, 51n8, 63, 111, 124, 140, 141
Efficiency, 6, 40, 62, 67, 112, 136, 155
Egocentrism, 122
Ego-oriented, 7, 96, 102, 103, 113, 124, 129, 152
Emotional load, 150
Environment, 5, 20, 24, 35, 44, 56, 77, 79, 84, 89, 108, 114, 116, 129, 130, 140, 153, 155, 157
Essential jobs, 4
Exchange economy, 6, 50

F
Facebook, 57, 58, 69n15, 100, 141
Family/partner violence, 4, 11n29, 28n15, 66, 150
Female-coded behaviour, 8, 110, 123
Feminised sectors, 26, 111, 112
Feminisms & Degrowth Alliance (FaDA), 87
First Nations, 13n53, 49
Foundational economy, 4, 140
Fragmentation, 46, 50, 129, 135, 158
Free market competition, 136
Frugal abundance, 78, 83

G
Gaslight, 55–68
Gaslighting, 67, 86
Gender, 4, 6, 8, 22, 27n1, 35, 44, 45, 47, 49, 50, 56, 58, 67, 69n16, 75, 78, 86, 94, 108–116, 122, 125–128, 130, 131, 141, 142, 151, 152, 155–157
Gendered ageing, 17
Gender equality, 141, 142
Generation Expendable?, 4, 5, 8, 16–27, 35, 37, 40, 44–46, 48, 55, 58, 67, 74, 88, 95, 96, 108, 129, 140, 150, 155
Gift economy, 5, 8, 47–49, 56, 58, 62, 65, 66, 68, 74–89, 94, 95, 99, 100, 102, 104, 113–115, 125, 130, 140, 143, 151–160
Gift-giving, 8, 47, 63, 77, 84, 95, 101, 102, 110, 113, 116, 125, 129, 158–160
The Gift Highway, 5, 48, 49, 58, 75, 96, 100, 125, 153, 154, 158
Gifting, 47, 48, 58–62, 64, 76, 77, 96, 125, 133n14, 153, 154, 157, 158, 160
Girlboss, 109, 111–113, 156
Global North, 8, 59, 83, 101, 109, 112, 116, 137, 138, 152
Global South, 49, 83, 142, 152, 157
Goettner-Abendroth, Heide, 8
Good Karma Effect (GKE), 57–59, 61, 64, 74, 75, 78, 79, 83, 84, 87, 88, 96, 99, 100, 104, 151, 153, 155, 156, 158

Good Karma Network (GKN), 58–64, 67, 68, 74–76, 78–84, 86, 87, 89, 90n13, 90n22, 91n26, 95, 96, 99–101, 104, 125–127, 153, 154, 156, 160
The great reset, 2
Great Resignation, 136, 140, 142
Gross domestic product (GDP), 48, 140, 142
Group administrator, 100
Growth, 2, 5, 7, 40, 48–50, 57, 59, 80, 83, 86–89, 100–102, 104, 109, 112–116, 122, 124, 127, 129–131, 139–141, 143, 152, 153, 155–160

H

Health, 3, 17, 19–22, 24, 27, 27n1, 28n17, 35, 44, 45, 74, 137, 142, 150, 152
Healthcare, 4, 19–21, 27n1, 29n24, 34, 51n8, 111, 140, 141
Hegemony, 101, 129, 139
Heuristics, 7, 74, 96, 151, 157
Hierarchy, 5, 7, 40, 49, 94–104, 108–111, 113, 114, 150, 152, 153
Hive mind, 62, 80, 81, 95, 101, 153
Homelessness, 4, 8, 17, 151
Horizontalism, 129
Housing precarity, 18
Hybrid work, 136
Hyper-local, 5, 56, 57, 61, 64, 89, 100, 104, 153

I

Imaginaries, 7–8, 78, 86, 100–103, 112, 114, 129, 130, 140, 153, 155–156, 158, 160
Imagination infrastructure, 2, 6, 101, 108, 114, 128–131
Inclusion, 82, 94, 154
Income precarity, 17, 18
Indigenous economy, 125
Individualism, 2, 6, 62, 65, 104, 122, 123
Inequality, 4, 46, 108, 113, 116, 128, 130, 141, 142, 157, 159
Institutionalism, 46

L

Labor process theory, 46
Labour, 3–6, 8, 16, 20, 21, 27, 40, 46–48, 55, 56, 58, 74, 83, 95, 100, 112, 122, 125, 129, 136, 137, 141, 142, 160
Leahy, Terry, 47, 79, 102, 159
Lean in, 141
LGBTIQA+, 113
Liberalism, 141
Liegey, Vincent, 83, 84, 100
Local exchange trading systems (LETS), 57
Localism, 79, 153, 160
Lockdown, 3, 19, 44, 51, 58–61, 64, 69n15, 74, 78–80, 89, 136
Lying flat, 137

M

Male-coded behaviour, 109, 112, 122
Male-dominated sectors, 136
Mann, Barbara Alice, 66, 67, 102, 124
Market, 3–6, 16, 21, 27, 40, 48, 56–58, 65, 74, 88, 95, 101–103, 110–112, 116, 122, 129, 130, 136–138, 153
Masculate, 110
Masculinity, 110, 122–129, 157
Material gifting, 59–60, 64, 125, 133n14, 153
Maternal, 68, 76, 77, 90n11, 102, 103, 110, 113–115, 128, 154–157

Matriarchal, 66, 77, 114, 115, 124, 151, 158, 160
Matriarchy, 115
Mauss, Marcel, 47, 102
Men, 3, 4, 8, 17, 22, 26, 37, 44, 66, 74, 109–113, 115, 122–125, 127, 128, 151, 154–157
Men as gendered, 110–111
Middle class, 139
Miles, Angela, 159, 160
Mobbing, 35, 86, 96
Money, 5, 7, 8, 48, 60, 64–65, 75, 80, 83, 96, 124, 125
Motherers, 76, 77, 103, 113, 128
Muthien, Bernadette, 115

N
Nelson, Anitra, 65, 78, 83, 84, 96, 100
Neoliberalism, 40, 58, 62, 111, 139
Non-masculine genders, 8
Non-material gifting, 60–61, 125, 133n14, 153
Nurses, 20, 41n4, 45, 136, 137, 141

O
Older women, 4, 16, 19, 20, 22, 27
Open-localisation, 78–79
Open localism, 78, 79, 82, 153
Open relocalisation, 78, 80
Other, 95, 104, 123, 131, 152, 154
Other-oriented, 84, 103, 151
Overwork, 140

P
Pandemic, 2–5, 7, 8, 11n27, 11n29, 11n30, 11n31, 16, 18–21, 24, 27, 28n15, 35–37, 40, 47, 48, 50, 51, 55–59, 63, 67, 69n15, 74, 75, 78, 79, 81, 82, 84, 87, 89, 90n22, 91n25, 91n26, 100, 101, 104, 118n26, 122, 123, 128, 129, 136–143, 148n57, 150–152, 154–156, 158–160
Pandemic frontline, 9, 44, 66, 87, 122, 137
Paradigm/paradigmatic, 2, 5, 7, 40, 46, 47, 49, 50, 58, 75, 76, 83, 88, 94, 95, 101, 103, 110, 112–115, 122, 124, 127, 131, 143, 152, 155, 159, 160
Part-time work, 18, 112
Patriarchy, 5, 40, 66, 112, 115, 124
Patri-colonial capitalism, 102, 110, 114, 154
Paulson, Susan, 142, 143, 158
Perpetrator, 26, 40, 41n2
Petrilli, Susan, 77
Pink recession, 4, 122, 150
Place-based, 153
Plasticity, 128–131
Platform-economy, 56
Polycrises, 2, 7, 8, 129, 140, 152, 155
Post-capitalism, 104
Power relations, 49, 113, 130
Profit, 7, 57, 79, 80, 82, 101, 112, 153
Pyramid of capital, 48, 113, 114, 116, 128, 150, 156

R
Radical selfishness, 122–128
Rage rooms, 137–139
R/antiwork, 139
Rational economic man, 102, 130
Real values, 65, 89, 96
Reciprocity, 47, 65, 84, 86, 95, 96, 102–103, 153
Reddit, 139, 146n38
Relational care, 64, 83, 113, 128

Rematriation, 103, 113, 114, 124
Remote working, 3, 136, 150
Reproductive work, 3, 110, 140
Retirement, 16, 18, 136
Risse, Leonora, 4, 56, 108–109

S
Screamatoria, 137–139
Second shift, 94
Self, 50, 111, 131, 154, 156, 159
Selfishness, 74, 129
Settlement, 45, 131, 150, 152
Sexism, 4, 140
Shadmi, Erella, 6
Shecession, 4, 74
Shiva, Vandana, 124
Single income, 18
Social cohesion, 151
Social glue, 5, 56–57, 84, 157
Subaltern, 155, 156
Subordinate, 26, 46, 94, 155
Sustainability, 65, 114, 158
Sustainable communities, 83
Systemic-disadvantage, 49, 116

T
Teachers, 5, 18, 20, 29n18, 115, 136–138
Teaching, 20, 62, 137
Technology, 57, 114, 136
Timebanking, 57, 69n11
Time pressure, 74
Toxic positivity, 96, 99
Toxic workplace, 5, 34–40, 44, 87, 140, 150, 151, 155
Transactional, 7, 48, 95
Transition Towns, 57
Trask, Mililani, 65
Truth, 66, 67, 124, 155

U
Unpaid care, 17, 56–58, 86, 89
Unpaid labour, 74

V
Vaughan, Genevieve, 47, 50, 75–77, 94, 109, 110, 112, 113, 130, 152, 156, 157
Virtual, 57, 61, 62, 64, 79, 80, 89, 100, 104, 153
Voluntary, 5, 56, 95, 96, 100, 127, 157, 159
Volunteering, 56, 155

W
Welfare, 142, 151
Welfarism, 40
Wellbeing, 19, 20, 44, 111, 138, 139
Women, 3–8, 11n29, 16–24, 26, 27, 27n2, 28n3, 28n5, 34–40, 44–48, 50, 51, 55–57, 62, 66, 74, 75, 84, 89, 94, 96, 101, 108–112, 114, 122–125, 127, 128, 131, 136, 140–143, 150–157
Worker resistance, 139
Workers, 3–5, 7, 8, 16–18, 20–24, 26, 27, 27n1, 29n24, 35, 40, 44–46, 48, 50, 56, 62, 63, 66, 67, 74, 84, 87, 88, 94, 96, 101, 109, 111, 112, 116, 122, 123, 127, 128, 131, 135–143, 150, 155, 157, 159
Working class, 137, 139, 142
Working from home, 19, 136, 138
Work/life balance, 19, 136, 137
Workload burden, 45, 150
Workplace, 5, 7, 8, 19, 21–24, 26, 27, 45, 49, 50, 58, 61–63, 67, 68,

75, 82, 84, 87–89, 94, 96, 99, 108–112, 122, 127–129, 137, 138, 140, 141, 143, 150, 152–157
Workplace bullying, 9, 24, 26, 27, 34, 35, 37, 40, 84, 94, 151
Workplace culture, 6, 16, 23–24, 26, 27, 34, 40, 49, 62, 67, 84, 108, 109, 125, 150, 155, 160
Workplace hazards/harms, 24–25, 27, 34, 66, 129, 150
Workplace sexual harassment, 45

The manufacturer's authorised representative in the EU is Springer
Nature Customer Service Centre GmbH, Europaplatz 3, 69115 Heidelberg,
Germany. If you have any concerns regarding our products, please
contact ProductSafety@springernature.com

Printed and bound by CPI Group (UK) Ltd, Croydon, CR0 4YY
06/10/2026
02225878-0002